I Am Love

Book 1

I Am Love

Book 1

First Edition

Written and designed by Paul West and Holy Spirit
Edited by Paul West, Holy Spirit and Triskana West
Photograph of Paul by Triskana West

Published by Forgiven Mind, Watertown, WI, USA
Website: **www.forgivenmind.com**
Email: **iamlovebook1@forgivenmind.com**
www.facebook.com/IAmLove.ForgivenMind

ISBN: 978-0-615-59713-3

For my beautiful love Triskana,
for my True Self,
and for every one who is Love
(that's you)

Contents

P_{art} 3

Contents

Introduction

I am a healer and this is my healing. I heal myself - I am everyone. I do this for all and not for another. We are all joined as One. I teach myself to heal through my willingness. I am willing to heal my mind. My friend Holy Spirit teaches me to heal as I allow myself to be healed. I and others are healed together. I am a teacher and a student. I am the healer and I am also healed. Holy Spirit shows the way.

I write with forgiveness to undo the writing. I teach to remove the teacher. I use this time to apply true forgiveness of myself and therefore everyone. I choose true salvation for myself that I may be truly an example of love. I have no audience that I need consider. I need not entertain others. My true relationship is between me and God. God is always within. I heal to heal my relationship with God, which from God's view is already healed. This is a reminder of who I am and what is truly real.

What I see within this book is only what I project upon it. I use it for whatever I choose it is for and see there what I have projected. This book is a process of undoing guilt. This book is my awakening. This book does not contain salvation or externally save me from death. It is not the source of truth. It is merely a useful illusion. It need not be followed or worshipped or obeyed. It does not dictate who I am. It merely might remind me of my True Identity if I choose to use it for this. It tells me I am God's holy Son and love is all that there is.

The value in this process is the forgiving, not the reading. The value is applying forgiveness. It is good for me to be willing to heal. It is good to allow what is real. This purifying commitment serves my awakening. It provides opportunities to heal. It lets me explore what's really in my mind. It opens the door to reveal. I go inside and find who I am. I do this just for myself. I don't have to worry what other's might think. I lay all my fears somewhere else.

God is my Father, Mother and Creator. I am an extension of love. I've never been sinful, guilty or hurtful. I am accepted by God. I let Holy Spirit write through me now. I let Him show me the way. I open to finding the truth that is here. I'm already love anyway. Peace is my being. Love is my life. Joy is my natural condition. I let the light shine to dissolve what is false. I need no-one else's permission.

I write for myself to remember myself. I write only what is truthful. I honestly claim my own divine power. I did all this and not another. I take back my notion of things happening to me. I undo my belief in death. I write with forgiveness to undo separation. I write with forgiveness instead. I'm here to be willing to accept I'm mistaken. I'm here to accept Holy Spirit. I'm here to allow love to show me the truth that I'm very much loved and safe.

I'm willing to heal. I'm willing to forgive. I'm willing to see death undone. I'm willing to be open. I'm willing to trust. I'm willing to see I am one. I apply true forgiveness to see with the truth that nothing has happened except love. Love is here and love is real and love is all I've done. I am not separate from God. I am not condemned. I only need awaken to love. I'm dreaming a dream of a separate life where impossible death is mistaken. I'm Immortal Spirit, created with love. My home is with God within. I trust I am led on a path of peace. I trust Holy Spirit, not sin.

All I need do is write down this truth and write down what I might hear. I only forgive to remember what's true and to lessen believing in fear. God is with me; I share in His strength. I share it to share it myself. I need not worry about what to say. Holy Spirit will write this as well. Holy Spirit, please take over. Fill my mind with what's right. Show me the truth that's hiding within me. Help me remember my light.

I let go and surrender my ego intentions. I let my voice be quiet. I step to one side and allow love to flow. The love is shining in silence. I am God's Son. I am God's love. I am God's extension of light. Holy Father, thank you for love. Thank you for all you've made right.

I am home in love. I am home in peace. I am home in perfect oneness. The world is undone. I am God's holy Son. Love is the truth. I am love.

$\mathcal{P}art\ 1$

Chapter 1

I am not a body

The body is not real. It's not even there. I think it's there because I made it up with my thinking. The body doesn't limit me or confine me or stop me from being who I am. I am the one who projected it from my mind. It came from me, and is in my imagination. It's just a dream, not a reality. I tell it what to do. I orchestrate everything it does. It is a puppet, empty and waiting for commands. I use it for whatever I choose. I can choose to use it for forgiveness. I can take the opportunity to remind myself that I am not this body – how can I be when this body is not even here?

I am Immortal Spirit, whole and holy as God created me. I extend God's love through this body that I may share in it and make it available to be shared by all. The body does not limit who I am or confine me to space or time. It has no hold over me.

I am free in Spirit. My mind is free of ego and this body is just a symbol of the ego, therefore I am free of both the body and the ego. It is not who I am. It is not my identity. I cannot be a bag of bones. I cannot die or be damaged. I am eternally alive.

I am guiltless. I have not separated from God and God has not been the slightest bit influenced by my misbelief that I have separated. I have not succeeded in pulling off separation from God. I have no need of a body to symbolize a successful attack on God, for God is not attackable. To think otherwise is insane. God has not been affected by my belief in the body being real. I have not been affected by my belief that I actually am this body. It is not me. I am God's Son, wholly loved beyond all separation and guilt.

Other people's bodies are just the same as mine – imaginary, temporary illusions in our shared mind. We hold them as images in front of ourselves and try to use them to prove that we are not one, but even a body cannot keep us from being as God created us. The body cannot do anything to God, to harm Him or influence His opinion of me. God did not create this body or anyone else's body. I am just mistaken with ego thinking when I believe the body is real. It is not real and never was.

I am not a body because I am not separate from my Creator. This flesh does not stop me from joining with others in mind and Spirit. It is not a barrier to love. It is incapable of forming a gap between myself and others or myself and God. The body has no power to do anything to anyone, even to myself. It has no will of its own. It has no agenda. It has no personality. It is just an illusion of wrong thinking. It can do nothing on its own and it never has. It has faithfully carried out my use of it, and my use of it can change at any time. I created it with my thought, and it is still in my thoughts, but not reality.

My body does not determine who I am. It has no causal power over me. It does not dictate my experiences, nor cause me to feel a certain way. It does not command me nor relay to me messages of truth from outside of it. It is a figure in a dream, it is not real and is in no position to tell me what is really happening. It is a part of the very dream I have been lost in, but that dream is no more real than my body. I am safe from the dream in God's arms.

This body tells me only what I have instructed. It does not know. It has not decided. It has no dominion or thought or mind or capacity of its own. It is only what I would have it seem to be in my mind, and only temporarily so. It comes and goes

21

and changes as I see fit, never lasting and never stopping to be completely still or real. It is a fleeting image in my mind. It is not who I am. I am love and I will always be love.

Peace is within me and is not disturbed by the presence in my mind of a body. The body does not hinder my peace nor stop me from dwelling in peace forever. It has not removed peace from my mind nor is it capable. It is nothing. It never was anything more than a thought. It has no causal power to adjust my reality nor change my experience. Its lifelessness affects me not. I am as God created me to be, by God's will alone, and I can't change that.

I am guiltless and sinless and forgiven. I have never done anything wrong. My body has never demonstrated evidence of my attack on another or of them upon me, for I am not attackable. I am the invulnerable Spirit shared in God's creation. This body is harmless, meaningless, guiltless, identityless and it is not who I am. I am only love.

I told this body to act according to my will. I put it out there. I projected it with my mind, in my mind and it has not left my mind. I imagine it to be what it is, and it appears so. I orchestrate its every move with my mind. I instruct it and arrange it and manipulate it. I feed commands to it and use it as I see fit. I can let the Holy Spirit use it for me to facilitate forgiveness of what never was. I don't have to fear the Holy Spirit's use of my body; it is gentle and loving and no harm will come from Him.

Whatever message this body appears to tell me, I told it to tell me. I put words in its mouth. I put sensations upon its skin. I filled its eyes with imagery and cast sound to its ears. It tastes only the world I feed it and moves only as I allow. It does nothing against my will. Like a puppet on a string I dangle it before myself, playing games of forgetfulness, making out it does this on its own. It is not even there.

I pretend to forget that I created the body in my mind, or that I tell it what to do. I come to believe wrongly it has power over me and commands me with its response. I make myself a victim of its responses to an external imaginary world. I make sure its messages strike me as real and play along as if I knew not they were due. I pretend to cut strings of control such that I may act as if the body has a life of its own. But it is pretend and I'm just fooling myself to think otherwise. It has done nothing to me against my will, ever, and it won't, ever again.

I don't have to use it the way I have been. I don't have to listen to my own instructions returning. I don't have to believe the lies in the messages, upholding views of what is occurring externally. Its messages are filled with my own stories, made up in my mind and told to myself. Who else is there to storytell? I have tantalized and horrified myself through these messages, not through their power to affect me but through my pretense that they have affected me. I agree with them, freely, to make it appear these messages influence me, but they are not causal and have no charge over me.

If I were to think otherwise, that the body's messages cause me not, perhaps I would realize and remember, again, I am love. Perhaps I would decide to recall the body is not capable of instructing me. Perhaps I would let go of my sleeping attendance to its mistaken perceptions and rouse a little into awakening. Perhaps then I would let go of being at the effect of what I truly am causing myself.

I am not a body, I am Immortal Spirit.

Chapter 2

I am not alone

I forgot I was one and believed I was many and few. Who am I? This separation isn't real and hasn't occurred. It's just my imagination. I can't be alone because my Father in Heaven is with me. I am one with His Creation forever. There is nowhere that He is that I am not, and cannot be away from His love. I am open to His immeasurable yet substantial offering of love to me. He created me with love, as love extended in joy. I am all-one with love.

Bodies keep me not from truth or joining. Others are not separate from myself. My separate self is not separate and others are not others. We are joined in mind and Spirit. Barriers and bodies do not deflect the love that I am from being real. I only imagine them to do so and pretend I can forget we all share in love equally. In truth we are all one and always will be so.

I am not alone because I haven't left Home, where God and I are inseparable. In Heaven we are one and there is no us, only what is. I was mistaken in thinking I could separate from God, given there is nowhere to go and nowhere to be that He isn't. I couldn't even go to a place other than where He is for He is infinite in His reach. So I pretended instead to divide God in half, that one part may seem opposite and different to the other, offering a barrier to devise a sense of separation. But God is not divided in His love for all, so I must be mistaken. God is whole.

Peace surrounds me because I have no enemy, no other and no separate identity needing defense from other separate identities. We are all together the same in mind and Spirit, not form. Who can be separate when separation hasn't happened? I am not isolated alone from Myself. How can I be not what I am? I can only imagine myself to be confined in an expanse of Spirit, pretending to hide behind walls and obstacles, identifying with those walls as if they are a semblance of self. They are not what I am, I am eternal and boundless Spirit.

I could only think I am alone when I already think I am separate, since only then is there something to be apart from. That is my error in thinking. Holy Spirit can correct my thinking to show me a way towards truth and remembering. Holy Spirit can direct me to see a world of only love as one. He can teach me these bodies and obstacles are not really there, not separating me from Myself or from Home. Only God is real.

There is no mistake, it is corrected. I am healed and whole as one Mind, one Son, one Holiness. All are encompassed in my being, lifted from darkness and rejoined in an expanse of mind. We are all here, together, blessed and basking in a sun of love. None are left behind, none are forgotten. Joy is here now, echoing to infinity and opening all to remember we never left. We've always been here, always a single being united in peace and reflecting God's love. What separation?

I rejoice now in a light of truth, a place of love and a peace of mind.

Chapter 3

I remember I'm dreaming

I'm dreaming. It's not real. It's just a dream. It isn't happening. I'm not really experiencing what I think is there. It's the illusion of something being there that isn't. I'm making it up myself and I'm imagining that I am a part of it. I'm getting lost in it, but it's only a dream and isn't real. I am not this dream. I am just the dreamer.

This dream is coming from me, including my body and all other people and places and things. These are all dreams, not realities. My mind is whole and one with God's mind, joined in Spirit as one. These dreams are not my reality and are just my imagination. I imagined this body, this world, this entire universe and I'm still imagining it now. And yet, I am just dreaming this.

It isn't a real dream, and I'm not really dreaming. This dream is just a dream. My mind is powerful in imagining what I think is real, and what I want to believe is real, even if it isn't. I've convinced myself that this dream is happening now, but it isn't happening now or at any time. It's in my mind. I am free from its effects. Dreams have no effect on who I am.

Since I am the dreamer I must be dreaming that I am a body, pretending I am a physical form in a physical world. I must be trying to pretend I am separate from all of the rest of the dream and that I am only one part of it. Yet there is only one dream, not many dreams, and what I call my body is no more mine than anyone else's. What I call myself as a body is no more me than anyone else, and all of our bodies are just dreams.

I am not part of a world I made up. I am whole, healed and holy, pure in mind and Spirit and joined in God as one. I am not subject to this dream or its events. I can't be because I'm the one who is dreaming them. They are in my mind, I am not in them. I am not inside a dream, I am not part of a dream, and I am not at the effect of a dream. I am the cause and I can choose to see that this dream is just that - a dream and nothing else.

I am the cause of this dream in my mind, in my imagination, and it isn't real. It stems from me and flows from me and is within me. All of the things I thought were happening to me, as part of the dream, by the dream, are not happening at all. I am not at the effect of my own long-forgotten causes. Nobody else is creating this dream other than me and nobody else is orchestrating what happens. I am not a victim of the dream I'm dreaming. I am the cause of my own imagining.

Since I am making all of this dream up myself, in my mind, I must be the one who is designing its every aspect, making it be what it appears to be and giving it a semblance of reality. There can be no other dreamer but the one who is dreaming, lest all our dreams collide and conflict. Our many dreams are not many but one dream, made up by one identity. Our dream is not any more real or important as one dream or as many dreams. All dreams are substitutes for real life. My life with God is real.

Nobody is doing this dream to me or forcing me to be influenced by its script. I wrote the script myself and put it into action, made it seem real and orchestrated its drama. There are no other separate minds willing against me or making me separate from them. Therefore this dream is by my own hand, being done by me not to me, and so any perception of it being against me is merely my forgetfulness that I dreamed it in the first place. I can remember now.

All other sources or seeming causes or influences or forces or aspects of power or will that I think are working against me are merely areas where I've forgotten that I dreamed this. They are merely opportunities for me to look differently to remember, with Holy Spirit, my True Nature, beyond the appearance of my forgotten power. Holy Spirit can show me the way to see how this body is not true, real, or who I am. I am not this body, this dream, this universe or these separate selves. I am as God creates me be.

All other sources and wills are guiltless, having caused not my experience nor influenced my will nor deterred me from my choice. They have no power over me and are not guilty of causing me anything at all. I caused the dream, I am the dreamer. The dream did not dream me. I am not the product of someone else's imagination or someone else's causal power. I was not born from a dream nor made from a dream nor dictated by the dream. The dream has no hold over me, who I am or my True Identity. It has not happened. I am Immortal Spirit, unchanged and free from imagining.

I am dreamless, guiltless and awake in God. Only God's world is real and true. Only light shines and has no dream to shine upon, for light shows that dreams are not real. There is no darkened dream of loss and attack, it is not there. My mind is clear of dreams, clear of pretense and clear from distorted illusions of fear. The Holy Spirit that I am is with me, within me, as me and through me. The clouds of dreams have parted and the sun of love is shining in my mind. I am free.

All those whom I thought guilty for attacking me are not causes in the dream and none of them are there. I made them up and animated them and dangled them as puppets before my eyes to blame them for what they have not done. I accused myself through them and hurt them with my forgetfulness. I dreamed of them as separate from myself and thus of myself as separate from who I really am. Thus did I forget I was dreaming and became confused in who is making dreams happen. But now I remember, it was myself, dreaming of exile in an imaginary landscape where the dream itself is my creator. I am created by God alone, always and forever.

This is the end of dreams. They were never there to begin with, just passing, fleeting ideas and images in my mind. I made them up and now they are unmade. My mind is clear with room for light to shine. Nothing has happened to muddy the river of God's love, running through my being, as me and with me. I am holy, I am love, I am real in God's mind and this is all there is to be. I am not a dream but a reality. I am only a reality, and God is real.

Chapter 4

I am innocent

I am innocent, having never sinned. Nothing has happened that shouldn't have happened, and I am not at fault. God loves me and knows my innocence is complete. I am holy, innocent, guiltless and sinless. I always will be so.

My innocence extends from God's innocence. God is holy, innocent, guiltless and sinless. God and I are both innocent because nothing has happened that God has not created. God creates from innocence and creates only innocence. Nothing else exists. I am completely innocent in the light of God.

All of the things I thought I did, did not really occur. I imagined them and brought them to life in my nightmare. Going all the way back to the seeming beginning of time, I am unaffected by any and all events. Nothing has occurred in the dream or in my mind or body or life, to me or from me. All lifetimes have been but a play of illusions in my mind and no real consequence has come from them. I am holy as God created me.

I am untouched by the world, unblemished by disaster and unscathed by death. All horrific nightmares have had no real effect on who I am. I am not defined by events or people or places or bodies or images or insane dreams. I am only what I truly am, which is God's holy Son.

My dream of murder and death has not been successful. I have not, in reality, accomplished what I thought I accomplished. I have not murdered God, myself nor anyone else. I am holy and innocent. God is still alive, perfectly whole, absolutely alight with living presence. Nothing I have ever done has harmed God in any way. God is completely unaffected by my mad dreams and still loves me.

I thought I achieved terrible results, instilling further guilt and damnation, demanding punishment, disease and death. Yet these were but dreams and I am not at the effect of a dream. My True Self is holy and always has been. My True Self cannot accomplish separation from God nor cause death to really occur. I am still alive in God's love forever.

All the things I did to myself and others have not been done. They did not occur. I was mistaken in thinking they were real or that they happened. I was faulty in perceiving them to be in the past, locked away in time and incapable of healing. Nothing has occurred that can't be healed, no sin nor death too final to undo. All is not lost. There is hope because none of this has happened. Only love is real.

I am at peace because I am God's holy Son, created to be holy forever. I am innocent because nothing can occur to prove otherwise. There is only one Son and no other to accuse or condemn me but myself. There is no counsel or group or person or being capable of choosing for me, against my will and against God's will, that I have succeeded in becoming guilty or have lost my innocence. My innocence is permanent and I am wholly innocent.

Being innocent I am incapable of anything but innocence. I cannot create separation nor produce a condition for sin to exist. I am incapable of death, incapable of murder, incapable of being where God is not. To believe I am guilty is an injustice because he who is innocent is incapable of sin. To accuse the innocent is to accuse unjustly, and all accusation is therefore unjust. Thus am I innocent - I cannot be guilty and I never have been.

I am as God created me to be. I am a shining example of pure and total innocence. I have no sin to hide nor darkness to conceal. I am wide open and sharing in God's total acceptance. I am here. I am alive. I am one with my Creator. We are innocent in truth and that is all I am.

Chapter 5

I am alive

There is no death. No-one ever died. There has not been an end to life. Life is eternal and I am Eternal Life. There is no punishment nor disease nor death. Separation has not happened and there is no loss. There is only life and I am alive.

Life is eternal. It has no end or beginning. Life has always been. God is life and God is eternal. God is not dead and can never die. God has not been lost and I am not lost to God. There is only a joining of life with life and I am perfectly alive.

Death and disease and destruction are illusions created by my thoughts. My erroneous thought system shows me images of death and ideas of death. Yet death isn't real. There has never been an end to life and all illusions of life are not real. Real life is eternal Spirit, joined forever in God's love, eternally sustained and always living. God's life is all that is.

Whomever I've lost or whatever has separated me from myself is not there. Whatever I thought I had which I appear not to have was not real. Nothing has been lost and no separation has come between me and love. I am love. I am and have everything that God created and need nothing else.

Ends are not final and are impossible. Illusions are always a continuum of change and changes never stop changing. They never really end because they're not real. They never began. Even illusions of ends are not final. I as one cannot end and have never ended. I am truly a continuum of living presence. I am alive.

Even my dreams of separation and death are not final. Even my seeming experience of separation and death is not final. Dreams cannot stop or truly be still, for they would cease to appear to be. Dreams can only show me transitions and transformations and stories of change, pretending to be a continuum. There is truly no absolute death in dreams or in reality. There is only life.

God created me and I am alive. God is perfectly alive and creates only perfect life. Perfect life is absolutely alive, immortal and invulnerable. Perfect life cannot be harmed, influenced, damaged, lost or ended. Perfect life shares perfect life with its Creator, as its Creator shares It's perfect life. I am perfect life and I share in perfect life with my Creator.

I have always existed as the One Son, an extension of God's being, within God's creation. I have never parted nor separated nor lost immortality. I am not a mortal body and I cannot die. My body is not life, it is an image pretending to be life. I am pretending to be a body pretending to be life and I chose to believe this is real. I can choose again. I allow the Holy Spirit to clear my mind and free my thoughts from the illusion that I am a mortal body. I am truly immortal and always will be.

Holy Spirit recognizes my immortality and shares it with me. Together as one we are holy and innocent, guiltless and sinless, harmless and dangerless, lossless and deathless, truly alive and truly united with our Creator. I am alive in the living love of God. God is real, God is life, and God sustains eternal life.

I am Eternal Life, peaceful and happy, free from death and immaculately pure. Nothing can touch me. Nothing is against me. There is only this loving life, in me and through me and everywhere. There is nothing else to be but God's living creation. I am forever alive in God's love.

Only love is real. Only life is real. Only God is real. Only Spirit is real. Only light is real. Only Creation is real. Only my True Self is real. Only the reality of love is real. I am the living expression of the reality of love in the heart of God and we are one forever.

Chapter 6

I am unafraid

Fear has no place in me because I am not fear. All fears are illusions in my mind. I make them up and make them real. I use fear to give others power over me. I act a victim through fear in order to see others as attackers. I displace my own power onto others and ask them to decide for me through fear. I let them choose my fate. I want them to do what I perceive them doing so that I can hide from myself and God. I have been afraid of God destroying me, enacting vengeance for what I've done. But I've done nothing but be love and God isn't out to get me.

I've used fear to pretend to be at the effect of other people and events. I've asked them to cause my experience and yet have been terrified at the thought of being at their effect. It is the idea of being at their effect that makes fear feel the way it does, because choice seems beyond myself. It horrifies me to think it possible that an alien will against my own could determine my experience. And yet by choosing fear I create the scenarios that scare me. I scare myself. Yet fear is but a tool for disowning my own power, and forgiveness is its undoing. I am forgiven of my insane obsession with fear and it is gone.

My fear always projects itself onto any available target, explaining and justifying itself with a pointing finger. It tells stories and creates distractions. It finds causes for itself and reasons why it is real. It tells me I am afraid for a myriad of reasons. But this conceals fear's grand deception, which is that without blaming others there is no justification for being afraid. Fear can do nothing when its great illusion is unveiled, and I am not afraid.

Fear itself is always a lie. I pretend other people are the cause and that I should fear those causes. But really to fear is to use others against myself. I use fear to cause an appearance to myself that others created my fears. My projection creates my perception. Fear justifies why I should listen to it and believe in it. It paints sorry pictures of terror that I will believe its story and deceive myself. Fear is not my ally. Fear does not protect me. Fear is never working for me. Fear is always against me, as it is always my way of working against myself. I need not be against myself in fear. I am with myself in love.

There is no reason to be afraid. All fears are invented smoke and mirrors. There is no enemy that I haven't envisioned. There is no threat I haven't devised. There is no one against me that I haven't split off from myself and accused. There is no separate cause and I am not at the effect of a scary nightmare. My fears are not true and I am not alone. Holy Spirit is here right now, holding my hand.

I can listen to the Holy Spirit's loving support all day. It is okay that I trust His gentle guidance. His counsel is sane and true. He does not distract me or deceive me like fear. He does not pretend He is caused by something separate. He does not need prove His reality by justifications and explanation. He is here with me in my mind and we are one.

All fear is gone and does not last. It comes and goes on a whim and finds sources for itself randomly. It is an insane projection of things not happening. Holy Spirit is correcting my thinking and removing fear from my mind. I do not need to do this alone. I do not need to confront my enemies or avoid them in fear. There are no enemies that I haven't made myself. I need not be afraid of what I myself have created.

I have only ever been afraid of my own imaginings. I have only ever used others to make myself terrified. I have only ever devised ways that others can seem to prove to me that my home is threatened. I have only ever used them to justify my belief in fear, loss and death. No more. I do not need to use them in this way. There is a better way with the Holy Spirit's help.

I take the Holy Spirit's hand and release myself from my dependency on fear. I choose not to listen to fear's advice and I follow it not. I have a new teacher, my old friend, my trusted partner and true comfort; a reminder of who I am. I am as God created me. There is only safety in God's arms and God is everywhere I am. I go nowhere without Him and He is with me. I am safe in God's love and protected from my own fearing. I let it go and I be at peace, still and thankful that fear is no more.

Chapter 7

I join with God

God is infinite love. I am in God completely.

I haven't created a separation between myself and God, it is impossible. I can't stop God from being what God is. I can't create a division in His being where there are two parts with differences. God is not different from Himself or apart from Himself. Separation within God has not occurred and never will.

Since I am God's creation, an extension of His love, I must be as He created me to be. I have no say in making myself be something God has not chosen. I have no ability to choose for God on His behalf or to decide for Him. I have no sway or power of decision to know anything other than God's will. It is impossible for me to go off on my own and be outside of or somewhere other than where He is. He is with me everywhere I am and I am never without Him.

God is everywhere. God is complete. There is nowhere that God does not exist. God's infinite being stretches far and wide beyond all boundaries and limits. There is no end to God, no stopping point or place of non-existence. There is nowhere to be and nowhere to go where God is not. God surrounds and envelops everything that is real forever. I am nowhere else but in God right now and this is the only way to be.

Separation has not happened. I have not found a hiding place where God is absent. I have not created a world outside of God's mind. I have not become something He did not will I be. I am the shining beautiful thought in His infinite mind. I am one with God and not apart. There is nowhere else I want to be. I am here with God right now and He is here with me.

I couldn't be separate from God because separation is impossible. There is nowhere beyond Him and nowhere beside Him. There is no other God or other world or other place to exist. I create illusions in my mind of finding other places to go and live without His love, but these are just dreams. They are not real. The physical world of form is not real and does not exist.

I am not trapped in a world of separation. I am not lost in a desert of unlove. I am not void of the living presence of God's life. I am not lacking His absolute sharing. I open myself to the absolute sharing and total abundance of God's willing love. I need for nothing but to be what I am as God's holy Son. I can be nothing else and nowhere else. I am only joined with my Father in heaven, once and for always.

Light fills me as I remember who I am, guided by Holy Spirit to recall my being and remember my home. Joy comes to me as I awaken to awareness of the ever-loving presence of my Creator. Happiness returns to me as I embrace the welcome that is here for me, the complete offering of acceptance of all that I am. I uncover my gratitude as I appreciate the utter love and knowing comfort emanating through me and around me. I celebrate the miracle that has guided me home to God.

I am here at last, at peace. I am joined at last, remembering no separation. I am present at last, knowing the past never was. I am restored to my True Identity as the total union with my loving Father. I am completely filled with God's being in my heart and in my mind, now and eternally. I am only this, God is only this, and we are together always.

Chapter 8

I am safe from attack

The world isn't real and imaginary people aren't capable of attack. I imagine only the consequences of attacks that aren't real. I make up solutions to imaginary attacks for invented reasons. I strive for outcomes and circumstances that are beyond my seeming control, wanting them to remain unsolved by denying my part in creating them. The world isn't real and I am not attacked by the world.

My brother does not attack me. Nor do I attack my brother. No consequences have ever come from our imaginary efforts to attack bodies. No life has ever been lost because bodies aren't alive. Bodies only appear in movies to play a part in being used for dreams of attack. Attack isn't real and can't be, because I am holy. I do not believe in attack and I do not attack myself. I am invulnerable.

All seeming attack is forgiven, having never occurred. Nobody has been harmed. There has been no loss or death or destruction. It's just a mad dream filled with deception and untruth. None of us are guilty for what has not happened. None of us have really attacked each other and no-one has attacked God. I am mistaken in my belief that I have attacked God successfully because God is invulnerable and immortal, as am I.

I am strong because I choose not to undermine my strength. I am not weak. I choose not to use the dream world against myself in stories of attack and defense. I cannot be attacked, I am Immortal Spirit. I cannot attack others and they cannot attack me. I cannot attack myself and I cannot attack God. Nothing has happened. There has never been an attack nor sin and no guilt is needed. We are all equally innocent.

I cannot attack because my Creator cannot attack and conceived only of life. Attack is an attempt to stop life, which is impossible. I cannot stop God from loving me. I cannot bring an end to life but in mad dreams in my mind. I cannot murder and have not caused death. I am pure as created from purity and holy as created by holiness. I need no guilt to remind me of what I have not done. I am free from guilt because God is.

I thought I attacked God and succeeded, but I was mistaken. I can do nothing but extend God's total love. I can be nothing but an extension of what God is. I can act only on God's will and God wills only love. I did not separate from God and I did not succeed in attacking Him. He is not going to attack me in return. We are not enemies, we are benevolent as one.

Since I did not succeed in attacking God, God is unharmed. God has never ceased to live and His life is completely free from attack. I cannot cause God, nor can I force God to be at my effect. I cannot make God be what God already is. I cannot decide for Him nor do anything to modify His will. I cannot inflict pain on Him nor deter Him nor hurt His everlasting being. I am completely powerless to stop God from loving me.

I have no effect on God except to share in God's love. I cannot change God with attack, sin or death. Nothing I have ever done or said or seemed to cause in illusions have ever affected God in any way. God has never had reason to retaliate nor judge nor condemn me. He has not rejected me. God has never pushed me away nor hurt me nor asked me to leave. God has never forced me out nor hunted me down nor sought my demise. God has no reason to because God is unhurt by my dreams of attack and God loves me. God has not changed in His love for me and never will.

It is only because I thought I truly attacked God that I think of myself as a body. It is only through my strong belief in having pushed God away that I believe I am distant from God. I invented this world in my mind as a place to pretend to hide from God's wrath, or from God's justified vengeance for what I did. But what did I do really? I did nothing. I have never truly done anything but be in God's arms of love, and God loves me.

I need not make a fake world seem real any longer. I need not use illusions to prove my attack on God and on myself. I need not pretend that others attack me beyond my control. I am not at the effect of attack and neither is God. Neither have I caused attack and neither has God, for attack isn't real. It has no power over me. I have used it to imagine what it would be like if attack were possible, and if it were so it would be a nightmare. But attack isn't real and has not happened. I am free from attack because there is none.

Without a made-up world to escape into, I need not hide from God. God is not out to get me. I need no world to live in alone. I need no world to remain without God's love. God only knows love for me and wants me with Him. God is not coming after me for things that didn't happen. God knows only love and is happy with me. God knows who I am and loves me greatly.

There is no world and I am with God. There is no attack and I am safe. I am safe because there is nothing to be safe from. I need not hide because I am not pursued. I need not fear because love is all there is. I need not delay for there is nothing to avoid. I am wholly in the arms of love and love is real.

Only God is real. Only love is real. Only God is. Only love is love.

Chapter 9

I forgive beyond time

I stand where time has finished and is no more. Time is over. Time never was or will be. I stand at the end of time and I have transcended time. I am timeless and ageless. It is not time for me to be awake, I am awake because there is no time and all time is sleep. I operate outside of time and move beyond its limits. I have limitless free time because I am free from time. I am eternal Spirit.

I look back from the end of time and see that nobody ever caused me harm. Nobody ever did anything to me that I did not want done to myself. Nobody ever caused events to happen beyond my control. Nobody that I ever blamed has ever done anything against me. Everything that I thought occurred in time has not happened. I am awake and time is over.

Anyone whom I thought to be the source of my pain or suffering was not the source. I was never a victim of anyone or anything. I only did to myself what I wanted to experience and even that did not occur. I am free. I am free from the past and free from time. I live in love and share love forever.

All are forgiven who thought they ever affected me. I blame them not. None of them ever inflicted suffering upon me nor caused me harm. I am not at the effect of a dream from the past. I only ever put myself to torture and self-suffering through my missed-creation. I learned every lesson and overcame every problem knowing there were none. I am beyond them all.

I forgive everyone for none have ever done to me what I thought. I have never been harmed and have never been afraid. I have never lost nor been alone nor stopped to die. I am free from dreams of death. Everyone I ever seemed to dance with in dreams are innocent and not bodies. Everyone I ever seemed to conflict with are innocent and not bodies. They are me. Everyone is innocent because dreams of time are not real and we are timeless as one.

I have never been in time nor on time. Time has no sway over me and does not confine me. My entire past was a fictional story of misbelief. I made it up. I persuaded myself to pretend to believe it happened. Separation has never happened and never will. Time cannot prevent me from being fully present now. I am here and God is here with me forever.

The Holy Spirit has cleansed my mind of mistaken thought and erased my false memories. My only true memories are of God. Even my memories of God are not real because I experience God for real now. I have no need for time nor history nor stories of old and new. Holy Spirit is in my mind and has restored me to my Complete True Self. I am the love of God.

My mind was filled with fantasy and now is quiet. I rest in God. I allow Holy Spirit into my mind to light the way and show how truly I am free from all illusions. I join with Holy Spirit now to allow Him to show me that I am beyond time and that time never was. Time is illusion and my mind is free from illusions. Holy Spirit is in my mind and always shows me only light.

I ascend into the arms of love knowing only that love is real. I let go of all histories of mistaken identity and all separations of unreality. God is the present focus in my mind always. I am a shining beacon of justice in recognition that all are holy as

God created. I am present and one with my Father, now.

I have never harmed another self for there are no other selves but me. I am unified and whole in my being and restored to awareness. I remember who I am and see myself as I am now. I am now who I have always been, beyond time and beyond death. I have always been here, present and still, truly alive and sharing in God's love.

All parts of myself are forgiven and healed. All aspects of mind are whole again. I need escape no more from nothing. God is real and I am infinitely peaceful. Nothing can change the peace that I am. Nothing can remove me from God's perfect creation. I am whole. I am healed. I am holy. I melt into the arms of love and remain in love forever.

I am eternally love. I am forever one. God is in me and I am here now at peace.

Chapter 10

I am without sin

Sin cannot occur because God is real. God is real and therefore sin cannot be. Sin is an idea of separation and I cannot be separate from God. God cannot be separate from me. Sin is the insistence that separation has happened, having happened not. Sin is impossible and has not occurred. I am innocent and holy and all is forgiven.

I thought I sinned because I thought sin was possible. I was mistaken. I thought I died because of sin. I was mistaken. I thought God ended because of sin. I was mistaken. I thought death was my only hope. I was mistaken. Disease, war, destruction, hate, pain, fear and all problems stemmed from my belief in sin. But I was mistaken for there is no sin and never was.

I have not sinned. Nobody has sinned because sin isn't real. We are all innocent and holy. Sin can be undone, having not really happened. I need only see the truth which shows me sin is not real. It is obvious to see sin is a fantasy and not my reality. When I see it clearly it holds no power over me. When I look with Holy Spirit's vision I see only that sin hasn't occurred. I am free from sin because Holy Spirit is in my mind always.

Sin is my insistence that sin is insistent. I used sin as my way to prove I succeeded in breaking away from love. I used sin as a weapon against God and myself. I declared war through sin and beheld death through sin and all love escaped me through my use of sin. I reflected belief in sin through many escapes and avenues, proving to myself again the sinner I thought I was. But I am not that. I am true and holy and forever will be as God created me.

I am able to see that sin is not real. I am capable of recognizing truth and knowing sin is not there. It never happened. I did not separate from God. I did not destroy Heaven or my Self. Sin is reversible, having never occurred. My belief in its reality is reversible. I can look again with new eyes and see that sin is gone. Sin is gone because Holy Spirit shows me the truth that there is no sin or punishment and only God is real.

I used sin to condemn myself to death. I used sin to destroy my integrity. Or so I thought I could, but

I am without sin

have not. Sin was my way to insist separation is possible. I waged it to certify separation as real. I made it my cornerstone of evidence and conviction. I let it be for me the nugget of irreversibility keeping me from love. I allowed it to dictate my guilt and orchestrate my fate. But sin is undone and is no more and I am free from guilt forever.

I am holy. Holy Spirit is with me. Holy Spirit is in my mind always, protecting my identity from false reality. Holy Spirit convinces me of truth because I can only know what is true. Holy Spirit knows who I am. Holy Spirit believes my innocence and never entertains untruth. He knows I cannot sin and am pure in God's creation. He holds for me the calm of my peaceful existence in God.

Never has sin occurred to keep me from my home. Holy Spirit clears the way for my mind to reawaken to love. I am blessed by His shining evidence of my true nature. There is no sin! It is undone and is not real. Guilt is no more because it is uncalled for. I have not sinned and need not suffer its consequences. I need not be concerned to undo the consequences by myself. Holy Spirit can correct all misdeeds and offspring from my erroneous belief that sin is real. I am freed from all responsibility to fix for myself what I have not done. I am not alone.

63

He is here with me in my heart and mind and always will be.

There was no sin. I am innocent. I am joined with God in a reunion of love. I never left home. I never broke away. I never stopped loving or being loved. God loved me to create me. I am created through love and holiness is my only reality. I could not sin and have no mark against me. All condemnation is unjustified and has no foundation. There is only God to base my Self on and only God is real.

I come from God and God flows through me. I extend from God's mind in a glow of love. I shine in His heart as a ray of joy. I am lifted to truth through His absolute knowing. I am alive. I am awake and I join my Creator in the eternal melody of light. There is only this. I am home and peace fills my holy being. I am here at last, where I always was and always will be, with my loving Creator.

I am without sin

Part 2

Chapter 11

I am free of dreams

I thought I was dreaming and dreamed alone. I lost my view of myself. I let go of my reality with God and pretended to sleep. I thought I could hide in my nightmare. I thought the dream was real and kept me from myself and my Father. I imagined untold miseries and mysteries and convinced myself of their existence. I purposefully wandered a weary path of nothingness. But it didn't happen because dreams aren't real.

I imagined myself to be something I am not. I thought of myself as bodies. I entertained dramas that couldn't happen and left myself no escape from death. I orchestrated romance and disaster, war and tranquility. I made images of life to dance on the stage and held their hand to move them. I wept at the loss of dreams no more and joyed at the arrival of dreams anew. I saw dawning and dusk of a million dreams and none of them showed me my home. I am with God now.

I couldn't stop the dreams I made for I believed they had sway over me. I thought them to be the cause of the body I dreamed and put myself at their mercy. And yet I used my bodies to put other dreams through death. I attacked and cowered, lost and made up, condemned and forgave. But amongst all these dreams I remembered not who I was really. I am the Son of God and God created me.

I am here with God now and dreams are not real. Dreams are only dreams, not real dreams. I dreamed them in my imagination and made them what they were. I projected their events and fantasized their climax. I did it all myself in mis-thought as I slept. I didn't realize I was the very one to birth them, and the very one to bring their completion. I set myself as the believer of my own misbelief and confused my vision of who I am. I am no longer a dream set on a fantasy stage, I am my True Self as love.

Dreams aren't real and haven't happened to me. I am not the result of a dream. I was not born from elements of dreams and did not die because of them. I never was the false identity I believed myself to be. Bodies aren't real and they were not who I am. Nothing happened. None of the stories occurred. None of the dramas nor their intermission. I am dreamless and real and filled only with God's living truth.

I remember who I am and I am not a dream. I can't be because God created me and not an illusion. I was not caused by a dream lest I claim I was caused by myself. I am caused only by love. Nothing then could occur to me. Nothing could condemn me nor torture me nor claim my death. I was the dreamer! By my own hand did I pretend to kill and be killed. By my own fantasy did I imagine my separate self real. But dreams of separation are not dreams of life and only God's is the life I live.

The nightmare is over and the Holy Spirit is with me now. I remember I am loved and have awakened to truth. My dream is over and I give it no regard. It is not lost and nothing of value ever came from it. I have sacrificed nothing to be as I am. No treasured toy nor specialized form ever had sway to tell me I'm unreal. I used them only against myself to pretend that God is unreal. Yet who can make God what God is not when God is what God is. God is, now and forever.

I have awoken from a nightmare that didn't happen. I have seen clearly in Holy vision that dreams can never occur. The nightmare was not possible. It was a dream of impossibility. Holy Spirit has cleared my mind of all erroneous perceptions and has undone my conviction that dreams are real. Dreams are not reality! My life as a body was not my reality. My life as a form was not my home. My life is with God in a shining miracle and I am one at peace.

I dreamed I was mistaken. I thought I dreamed and I did not. I thought I really separated. I thought I made a billion mistakes and deserved a terrible end. But shards of dreams are but glimpses of my only mistake, now undone and cleared with light. My only mistake is thinking I could be separate and dream my own world to live in. I cannot dream. I cannot make real what is not. I cannot tell God His truth. I cannot put before Him a dream of heaven to replace His own. What God has put in place I can put not asunder, and I thank God His world is real.

I am dreamless and bodiless and formless and lossless and deathless and tireless and diseaseless and painless and harmless and egoless and dreamless and completely free from all dreams forever. I join with Holy Spirit now to cleanse my mind of dreams I made real and release me from my own mistake. I deserve no punishment or further dream to claim vengeance for my error. I only need let go of dreams and fantasies and allow what is true to be. I am love.

I be love. I echo God's heart and mind. I am holy. I am real. I share in the abundance of my Creator. I am blessed with immortality. I am one with my Creator. I am innocent, happy and filled with reality. My mind is satisfied and absorbed in God. I need no more and have no other urge. I am found in the light of truth in my mind. I am home because God loves me. Love fills my being and touches my heart and this is all there is.

Chapter 12

I join with my brother

My brother and I are not apart. We are not bodies kept alone. We are not separate in our minds or hearts. We have not separated from home. We are not lost in the wilderness of private thoughts. We are joined and unified as one mind in God.

All separation is not real and I have not separated from myself. I thought I split off parts of myself to create the illusion of others. I thought I could take parts of myself and disassociate from them. I thought I could label parts of myself as others and give them names, and set parts of my will against itself. I thought I could make them act independently from me and orchestrate my future. But this I have not truly accomplished and separation is not real. We are a whole.

I took myself and split myself up to devise a multitude of selves. I scattered them seemingly far and wide through time and space. I pushed them out of my mind and beyond my remembering. I placed them as strangers on an ocean of dreams and left them there to die. I thought myself one of the multitude and not its origin. I swept aside my true nature and delved into the identity of a single instance, split apart. I forgot who I was, and I forgot they are me. Now I am restored to True Identity as Christ.

I used separation to create walls between my selves. I used fear and attack to strengthen the appearance of division. The more I hated toward the other parts of myself the more I thought this part escaped the hatred. That's what those parts thought too. I projected guilt from this part onto those parts and kept imprisoning myself. I didn't realize I was hating aspects of my own being. I used attack to condemn what I thought were others, reinforcing the perception that they are not myself. The more I pushed them away the more I could seem to forget we are joined. The more I hated them the more I forgot myself. Yet we are all joined in the peace of God and God is our home as one.

I imagined myself to be one of many. I am not many, I am one. I thought myself to be lost and alone. I am not alone, I have found myself. I recall with Holy Spirit's help that my dream of many selves is not my reality. I recall through His remembrance that all my brothers are but aspects of my own Self. To condemn them is to further pretend I can take myself from God. I cannot remove the identity that God has created. I can only be as God intended.

I join now with Holy Spirit in remembering who I am. I let go of the divisions in the landscape of my mind and see all selves as one. We are not apart, we are not many or few, we are all one. I see with Holy Spirit's vision that I have never succeeded in separating myself from myself. I see with Holy Spirit's help that I have never separated from my Creator. I recall my True Identity as God's holy Son and awaken to His loving presence.

Separation is not real and I am not separate from God. Separation is not real and I am not separate from myself. Separation is not real and I am not in a state of separate otherness. For all whom I thought other than myself, I remember our union. All whom I pushed away I welcome with open arms. I open to allowing myself to be the love and truth I am. I lift the veil of untold tales of otherness, blame and scam. I am whole again, healed in the light and living beyond the dream. I know myself to be myself and oneness is all that's seen.

I am one. I am whole. I am as God created me. I accept my True Identity and see it everywhere I look. I recognize myself in the pieces of Self I scattered. I see past the barriers and look past the bodies to see we are indeed all one. I am truly whole and complete, wrapped in light and clothed in love. I will always be the holy wholeness that God has created me to be.

Chapter 13

I welcome God's peace

War has ended and is no more. It never was. Peace exists, here and now. I am surrounded only by the loving presence of my Creator. I am an extension of peace. Peace is all I want and all I have. There is no disturbance or problem to fix. There are no worries or concerns or things gone wrong. Nothing is out of place. Nothing needs attending to. There is no work to be done. All loose ends are completed. All loss has been corrected. Everyone is reunited in a wholeness of love. All wounds have healed and all damage is undone. Here there is only the peace of God.

I believed in war and ends and sacrifice and let it run my mind. I used conflict to separate and openly welcomed my destruction. I wanted to destroy myself. I wanted loss and pain and agony over and over again. I didn't believe myself worthy of forgiveness. I thought I'd sinned forever. But I was simply mistaken. There is no war. There has been no loss, end or sacrifice. No love has died. Love is alive and I am alive. All are one, joined in peace, and peace is of God always.

I welcome the peace of God for it offers me sanctuary. I welcome peace of mind for it satisfies my needs. I allow there to be nothing that I want or need other than God. I let the presence of stillness touch my heart and fill me with rest and calm. I am at peace. I relinquish all worries. I give up all thoughts of my own. I surrender to the ever-present love. I let myself receive God's love and allow it to flow through me. I let myself be loved. I let there be love and let there be peace and peace is all there is.

All noise has gone away. There is calm and rest. Everything has settled. All turbulence has melted into calm. I relax and let go. I soften and trust I am supported. God loves me! There is love here now, with me. It fills me and surrounds me. I am worthy of this love and I let it love me. I allow love to be here now. I love myself by allowing God to love me. I can allow myself to love because love is all I need. God loves me now.

Peace fills every part of my being and washes away all thoughts of concern. The rough landscape of my mind melts and soothes and gives way to a mellow tranquility. There is calm here now. There is quiet. My mind is still and needs to go nowhere. I give up all worldly concerns, worries and doubts. I put all of this into the hands of the Holy Spirit to manage for me. I don't have to carry the weight of the world on my own. He is here, and I can let go.

Holy Spirit help me now, take into your hands my concerns. My trivial thoughts, my addictive worries. My constant condemnations. Take all of this from me and melt it away in your loving innocent light. Soothe all the aches and pains and upsets in my mind. Calm my perception and unjudge what I have attacked. Clear my mind of all self-guilt and bring out the sunshine of love. Shine on me, shine though me, let me rejoin you in peace. I can trust you Holy Spirit, now and always, to be the light in which I rest.

I let go. I let go. I let go and allow. I release the world and let it be. I don't need it to be the way I think. I let go of all requirements and expectations. I release it and let its myriad forms be as they are. I stop fixing. I stop solving. I stop seeing problems. I stop judging things as wrong. I don't know how anything should be. I can't correct anyone or anything. I need Holy Spirit to guide my thoughts and I allow Him to guide me now. Holy Spirit fill me with peace and restore my mind corrected. I let go and allow you to help me now.

I let go of the world and let myself be. I let go of attacks and let myself be. I let go of judgements and let myself be. I can be as I am without self-abuse. All around me is peace and light. All through me is peace and light. I ease and relax into the loving calm of God's love. I let myself go and trust I am safe. I welcome the peace that is here for me. I welcome the peace of God and let it be here for me. I am at peace in God forever and this peace is my home.

Chapter 14

I am the truth I seek

The way to truth is the way to myself. All of my searching has been for myself in God. God is truth and truth is all I have sought after. My searching has led me over hills and valleys, mountains and oceans. I could not find truth in a dream because a dream is not truth. Only God is real and only God is truth. I can find the truth in God.

I looked for truth where it is not and I didn't find it there. I looked there so that I would not find it. I knew it was not there and yet I looked there. I look there because I don't want to find truth. I don't want truth because I think the truth will kill me. I want to avoid truth because I am afraid of love. Yet I am not threatened by truth and truth is my safe home in God.

I have looked for an answer to a multitude of questions. I have pondered the meaning of existing-seeming events, trying to find truth. But there is no truth in made-up meaning. There is no truth in lies. All my questions are assertions of what I believe is true. All my questions are a rejection of answers. I did not want to find the answer to my problems. I did not want to find out that I am God's Son, but I am.

I lost myself by seeking for answers where they are not. I pursued dreams and fantasies that weren't real and escaped into them with assertions of what I wanted to find. I projected my thought and beheld it, to convince myself I am a separate self. I hid the answer and meaning from myself so I could waste time pretending to want other answers. Yet I did not want them and my search has always been pushing answers away. I can accept the truth now and allow the true answer in my mind.

I am not alone in my pursuit of meaning. Meaning is given me by my Father. Truth is meaningful because it is real. Truth is meaningful because it is love. All of my searching has been an unfinding of truth. I did not really want to find an answer. I did not really want to solve a problem. I made my problems real and bought into my own assertion that there are problems to solve and answers astray. But there are no missing answers and no problems to solve, because love is real.

Holy Spirit is here right now. He is in my mind showing me light. He fills my mind with illumination so that I may see all that is. The answer is all that is. Love is the answer. In the light of truth I can see clearly what is real and what is not. In light I am aware of every aspect of existence. In the light of the Holy Spirit I am free to be myself, one with my Father.

I invented darkness so that I could not see. I made up fantasy images to block my mind from love. I put obstacles and confusions in my path to deter me from awakening. I held onto illusions to keep me from reality. I defended myself against what I wanted to think was a terrible fate. I protected myself from love because I wanted to think love was as wretched as my protections. I saw only hinderance to my awareness of love because I hindered my love with illusions. All of these blockages to my awareness of love's presence are now lifted with the light of God.

I can see in light because light is whole. I can see in light because light shows me what I can see. In light, no part is kept apart or made darkened. In light, no part is mysterious or hard to see. When seen in a clear light, I can clearly see what is really here. What I thought was there was never there. I was very mistaken in thinking and believing in dreams of death. In light there is only an awareness of love.

All of my dark nightmares were dreams unreal, distorted perceptions of mind. Their images distracted and their lies deluded. I chose to think I was deserving of death. I chose to think I didn't deserve love. I thought I sinned and was guilty. I believed I had reason to fear. I thought things were happening beyond my control. I thought it was hopeless to defend against God's revenge. But God isn't vengeful, God only loves and God is here to love me now.

I only believed in the dark of my mind because the light seemed obscure and absent. Who can see in the dark? In the dawn of my reawakened mind I see all there is to see with Holy Spirit's true vision. With His vision, light shines on all the parts that were darkened and they are light again. All the corners and all the aspects of everything I couldn't see have been brought to illumination. I can see clearly in the light of the Holy Spirit and light is my only truth.

How obvious it is to see harmlessness now that light shines to show me the truth. How obvious it is to see nothing has gone wrong, nothing is broken and no consequence has come from a dream of separation. There is no separation here. It hasn't happened! Light within shows me a forgiven world, a world without sin or hate. This forgiven world was always here, covered over with fear and darkness. I can remember now that I mistook dark shadows as meaningful reasons to fear. I can release now all fear to the Holy Spirit and let Him steady my thoughts.

In light I see. In love I heal. In peace I restore. In God I rest. My mind is open to see again. My heart is open to love again. Truth was always here in answer to the lies. Separation has not occurred. There has not been a terrible dream made real. There is only a continuation of the love which God is. I am a continuation of God's love and I accept the answer that the Holy Sprit has for me. His answer is true, His answer is plain. I am innocent and holy and all is forgiven and released.

I join with Holy Spirit in remembering my truth, that I am the truth, the way and the light. The truth is within me because I am the truth. I am an extension of God. God's truth radiates through me. Truth is my very soul. I am the living truth that God is love and God fills me with Himself. There is only truth in my mind and only love is real. All is as God created it to be and I am as God created me in truth. The answer was always here, that I am God's holy Son, immortal forever.

Chapter 15

I give ahead of time

My giving is present. My giving is now. My giving is more immediate than delay. All of time is delay and is not now. I give ahead of time, all the time and time never touches me. I give before time so that time cannot be. I extend eternal thanks to my Creator so that I may be free from time forever.

Time is an illusion. It is past and future and everywhere but here. Space is time, and distance is time. The further I am away from here the more I am lost in time. The less I am here now the more I am in the past or future. Yet time is an illusion and has no power over me. I use time as a delaying maneuver to avoid myself. I avoid myself only because I think I killed God. It hasn't happened and I need delay no longer.

I extend God's love proactively. I don't stop, I allow the flow. I let it be what it is. I let God be in me and through me. I radiate my true nature as God's Son.

Upon encountering an illusory world, it is met with my proactive giving. My fore-giving shines light ahead on the road and casts aside all darkness. I proactively fore-see light all around me everywhere I go. I and all are forgiven.

I need not wait for murder or death before I attempt forgiveness. I need not delay in time before forgiveness is applied. I need not wait to make real a problem before I attempt to undo it. I must remember it is undone already in the light of my fore-giving. I already gave, even if I wasn't aware. I already extended God even if I thought otherwise. I need only become aware again that all is already forgiven in my mind and I am healed.

I meet illusions with light. I extend beyond fear with love. I shine away all dreams and unrealities. I open to reveal true existence. God is here. God shines a beacon that extends beyond all limits. God opens my mind to show me who I am. I am still the same as I was when He created me. I am still the love of God.

Time cannot distract me from who I am. Time cannot take away anything from me. Time cannot destroy my peace of mind. Time is an illusion that I created. I created time to pretend that delay was possible. I pushed imagined sins into the past to anchor them beyond correction. I demanded present guilt, derived from the impossible undoing of sin. I feared future destruction as warranted punishment for my inescapable guilt. And so I had no where to go. But none of this is real. Time is an illusion and I am the one who uses time against myself. I am free from time now and forever.

I choose now to extend the truth before the false can take hold. I choose now to join with Holy Spirit in my mind. I join with you Holy Spirit, take my hand and remind me of who I am. I am truth and light. I extend the peace of God everywhere I go. I am the living presence of love in God's heart. Holy Spirit clear my mind of all illusions of time and history and future illusions. I am here now with you.

I forgive to undo what has not been done. I forgive that lies can never begin. I forgive lest I forget to forgive and have to justify my failure. I give before, knowing I project my inner truth. I see what Holy Spirit shows me. I look upon the world, judging it not, remaining a light for truth. Holy Spirit helps me to see with clear vision. Holy Spirit helps me to know I project what I see. Holy Spirit presents the awareness that I can choose to see a forgiven world. Holy Spirit forgive the world through me and let me remember my home.

I join with God and allow myself to be what I am. I step outside of time and space and dwell in the timelessness of love. I be here now and always. I radiate and extend only true being and ask for light to shine through me. I allow myself to represent what is given already by God.

God already gave me. God already shone a light. God already created me ahead of time. God already looked with love. I am innocent because God knows nothing else happened. I am innocent because God extended Himself for me. I am safe because God is present here now. I am healed because God is all around me. I am not alone. I lift up into the arms of my Father and rejoin with Him in peace. I rejoin with you Father and extend love to you as you extend that love through me. I am a radio for your love and I broadcast for all to be.

I am here now, one and silent, lit and illuminated, restored to sanity and healed throughout. All dreams are gone now and love is all that remains. I be still and know that God is with me. I am home.

Chapter 16

I have no problems

I am tempted to believe something is wrong. But nothing happened. I'm inclined to think I did something wrong. But I didn't. I thought I made a real mistake. But I was mistaken about that also. There is nothing wrong and nothing has happened. All problems were made in my mind.

I entered into doubt and questioned my identity. I questioned God. In a questioning thought I invented unknowing. In doubt I feared that illusions were possible. I made up a world and gave it meaning, a world of separation. But this world does not exist but in my imagining. I can't live in a world that isn't real. I live in God in truth.

Questions gave rise to the impossible. I asserted that answers were impossible. I asserted that confusion is my answer. I hid from the answer in my mind. I hid the ability to know truth. I distanced myself from reason and illusions began to look real. All illusions began to look like problems because I brought truth into question. By doubting truth I made lies real and true answers impossible. By believing lies I could find no solutions. I did not want to find answers or solutions. I wanted my problems to stay. But I have no problem with God.

I thought I could solve problems on my own. But to be a separate self I withdrew from the answer. All aspects of the world appeared as a problem. There was something wrong and I had to fix it. But I've already convinced myself that problems are real. I already projected them and perceived them. I already made them by questioning God and want them to remain unsolved. Illusions will always seem like problems without God's answer. God is here now and His answer is in my mind.

I convinced myself I'd separated from God and made existence a problem. I convinced myself the problems were real and forgot I made them up. I bought into my own deceptions. I believed my own lies. I let myself follow my thinking and told myself problems are real. But illusory problems cannot be real because they don't exist.

I believed in real problems to believe in separation. There is no answer to separation if separation has happened. I cannot choose between this or that when the options are incomplete. I've chosen to keep things separate so I can keep finding no way to solve them. But there is no truth in an illusory world. I allow Holy Spirit to show me how these problems are solved and to show me how I am mistaken.

Problems began in my mind and that is where they are solved. The problem is not a projection of questions, the problem is my belief about God. I am perceiving a world that's not real and I am showing myself illusions. I show myself the form of problems to make decision impossible. Who can choose between unreal options? Who can say one is better? I gave all illusions the meaning they have so I can pretend to prefer one or another. But there are no sane choices in a world without meaning. The only sane choice is for love.

I need you Holy Spirit to correct my perception and undo my mistaken thoughts. I cannot tell what to do because I am showing myself what isn't there. I cannot decide between insane alternatives. All of my illusory options are insane. I cannot choose one or the other. My only choice is you. Help me Holy Spirit. Help me to see again. Show me the truth beyond impossible mistakes and remind me that love is real.

These mistakes are not out there. These illusions are not out there. These seeming choices are not out there. There is no decision to be made between them that could make sense. There is no value to one over the other. There is no right path to take. Nothing has been brought into question and there is nothing to choose between. Truth already is. I already am. Peace is in my mind and the answer is in my mind.

The real problem is my way of thinking. My perception just stems from my thoughts. I perceive a world of impossible choices when my mind has doubted who I am. My mind tries to bring God into question and that is my only problem. If I could see that God is not questioned I could see the truth again. If I could let myself open to the light I could recognize these problems aren't there. I open myself to you Holy Spirit, show me truth in my mind.

God is not in question. God cannot be questioned. God is not questionable. God is certain of love. God is the answer and I have no question. There is no problem to solve. There is no divided world to choose from. God is whole and God is real and God is with me now. There never was a question to ask. There never was a doubt. There never was reason to think of God as something other than He is. I am only as God intended me be and God does not question or condemn me.

There are no problems to look upon because God is what God is. There are no impossible options presented because God is the only way. There are no illusions to choose between because God is the only reality. I need not even make a choice to remember that God is God. God is already God in my mind and I share in God's love eternally.

I did not create you, Father, and nor can I take you away. I did not give you your nature and nor can I remove it. You are love and always have been. I have changed you not at all. You are peace and always have been. You are with me and always will be. You are here with me right now.

In your love and light I have no concerns. In your peace and love I don't worry. In your joy and light I can see the truth. The answer was here all along. The answer is in my mind where you placed it. The answer is "Love is real." Thank you Father for loving me so, and knowing that love is, still. Love is the only solution and love is all I need. Love is the only outcome and love is the perfect answer. Love is my strongest ally and love is the right path to choose. Love is the answer to all my imaginings for love is what I am.

I am free from false perception. I see only light and truth. All of my problems are solved because there are none. I am free of problems forever and I join with God in peace.

Chapter 17

I am worthy of God

Guilt has been undone. I am worthy of God. I was always worthy because of who I am. I have not sinned and God is convinced of my value. He has not changed His mind about me. I am His beloved Son.

I thought I did a terrible deed. I imagined a horrible end. I feared I'd lost what was once my own. I thought death was real and inevitable. I imagined all things ending with disaster. I feared the most that God would not love me. I thought I was far from home and banished from God's heart. I was clearly mistaken.

I thought God hated me and I believed I was worthy of hate. I thought I hated God. I thought God would strike me down and enact His revenge permanently. So I ran and hid in an illusory world I made up. I thought God would not find me. I shut out from myself all remnant of God to try to avoid my own death. But it was this very avoidance and hiding which made death seem so real. I cannot die an illusory death when God holds me in His heart.

God is my source and God knows I'm alive. God created me from Himself. I am the extension of His meaning and value. I cannot be a sinner to be hated when separation isn't real. I must be what He has created me to be, lest I be something I made. Does God really want me dead? Does God really deem me unworthy? No! God knows I am love and God could not hate with love.

Nevertheless I deemed myself unfit to live with God. I thought myself into disaster and enacted disaster upon me. I thought I deserved God's condemnation and condemned myself to death. I thought I deserved all punishment and made sure to make it happen. I really believed I deserved only hate and that love would never consider me. I thought love was dead because I thought I killed it and was left with guilt and death. But God is alive and God is love and God can only love me.

I was mistaken about myself, for thinking I was doomed. I was clearly misthinking when I imagined a world where my end would be played and repeated. I am worthy of God! I am worthy of God's love. I was mistaken to think I could change God or harm God. I was mistaken to think He was dead. I did not kill God and couldn't change His mind. He still loves me and holds nothing against me.

God is my Father and I am God's Son. I am the extension of His love. I can only therefore extend His being and represent the love in His heart. How can I be unworthy when I am made from worth? How can I be less or diminished when He knows my full identity? I am God's holy Son. I have not sinned and I am not guilty. I am worthy of love from God. I am worthy of being His Son.

Holy Spirit, join with me and help me correct my thinking. Help me to see that I am not unworthy. Help me to recognize truth. All of my sense of not being enough was alway my assertion that I wasn't. What if God could take a moment to answer for Himself His response? Perhaps I've been spending all this time so certain that God has rejected me. Maybe I haven't stopped to listen to hear what He has to say. Have I really sinned? Am I really guilty? Did I really harm God? Have I really pushed God away? Is God really my enemy? Does God still love me?

God does love me. God is not my enemy. God is not against me. God finds me worthy. I was wrong about God. I did not know what God's answer would be. I did not understand His answer. I could not bring myself to forgive my own self hatred. I only hated myself. God did not hate me at all. God does not hate me at all. God is only able to love me and all this time I haven't allowed it. I wanted to be unloved because I wanted to be separate and unique. But God loves me completely and recognizes my Self as His Son.

I am not alone anymore because God loves me completely. I am not unworthy now because I will let God decide my value. I put myself into your hands Holy Spirit, help me remember my worth. Help me remember my value has never been brought into question. I was mistaken for believing myself unworthy. I was mistaken for thinking for God. I was wrong to try to make His decision. I was so convinced I knew His response would be rejection. I thought He would abandon me again. I thought He would turn away and never accept me. But I am not capable of deciding for Him and I need not fear His decision. He knows who I am and knows my true nature and knows that I am love.

I let you decide for me Holy Spirit. Please clear my thoughts. I let you into my mind and heart and trust you with my life. I let you remind me what God's answer is. I let you determine my future. I allow you to help me to be here now and listen for God's response. I am worthy! I have done nothing wrong. All is forgiven and let go. It did not happen and was just an idea. It wasn't real and has not occurred. God loves me and I am worthy of God's love!

God, I know that you love me and I was mistaken for thinking otherwise. I know I am your holy Son and always will be in your heart. I allow you to fill me with reassurance that you will not reject me. I allow you to show me your true response and help me to trust you again. I let you lift me into your arms and fill me with your love. Thank you for loving me, God. Help me to be with you again. Fill my heart with your living love and correct me from thinking otherwise.

I am worthy of the love of God because I am His Son. I am worthy of the love of God because God created me whole. I am worthy of the love of God because I am the love of God. I am worthy of God's embrace because I am holy and innocent. I am worthy of the love of God because only love is real. I can smile in knowing that God loves me because love is the only truth.

I was never condemned and never rejected. I was never left alone. I have always been here, wrapped in God's love. I just forgot for a moment! Dreams are gone and love is here and that is all that remains.

Fear has left and peace has arrived and I rejoice in knowing I'm saved. I accept my value as the Son of God and I accept my place in His heart. I accept I am worthy of love and will never be apart. Thank you, thank you, thank you.

Chapter 18

I am joined with God

God is near, not far. God is here, not there. I am not alone. I am not lost. I am not afraid. It is safe for me to be with God.

God isn't going to hurt me. God isn't attacking me either. God doesn't hate me and God isn't an enemy. God is only love.

I am holy and innocent in God's eyes. God created me whole and innocent. I am forgiven having not separated. I have not ever sinned. There is no reason for me to not be with God. I have every reason to join with God and share His peace. I already am with God and God is with me now.

I thought I went far away in a long lost loveless land. I travelled oceans and mountains running away. I thought God would hunt me down and never take me back. I was alone, separate and condemned. But God didn't condemn me. God is only capable of love. God didn't reject me. God is only capable of acceptance. God didn't push me away. God is always welcoming. I have the opportunity to return to God in peace.

I ran away because I thought I sinned. I ran away from home. I thought and imagined a horrific thing and fled from certain punishment. I hid from God in the jungle of my mind. I couldn't find my way and I had nowhere to go but temporary hiding places. I thought I was hiding from God, but God was always with me. I thought I was succeeding in keeping Him away, but I was always being loved. God surrounds me with love and holds me in His heart forever.

I foolishly turned away in guilt thinking I'd done God wrong. I thought I attacked Him and took everything away from Him. I thought I destroyed Him forever. I thought this could not be undone and I thought I was doomed to die. But God was completely unharmed by my illusions and never once judged or condemned me. God didn't for an instant consider me guilty. God always knows I am love. Why would I think otherwise? I really can only be love.

I must have condemned myself. God didn't do it for me. I must have believed God was angry, but God isn't angry at all. I must have chosen to trick myself into thinking God would get me. But God was never looking to get me, only to love me completely. I used God as a scapegoat. I wanted God to be the one to reject me, so that I could blame Him. But if God didn't cast me away, I must have cast myself away. If God didn't unlove me, I must have unloved myself. If God didn't condemn me to death, maybe I destroyed my own life. Maybe God isn't mad at me after all and I did this all to myself.

If I did this to myself, then I surely am mistaken. I am trying to convince everyone I am guilty. But really I am trying to convince myself. I wanted to believe God was guilty so that I could be separate. I am not convinced, deep down. Deep down I know we are innocent. I can't seem to quite convince myself that God is truly my enemy. Deep down I can't quite believe that I've really separated from Him. I can't quite believe my own lies and assertions that I did something terribly wrong. I try and try and cry and cry but God still loves me all along.

What if I stop and entertain the idea I am loved? What if I drop the false belief that I did something I should've have? Maybe then God would accept me and pardon me for my sins. I still believe I've committed a crime and am sentenced to death forever. But I'm not. I am loved. I have not sinned. I am not guilty. I don't have to make it up to God because I haven't really done anything wrong. God is love and God is real and God already loves me completely.

Holy Spirit, correct my misthought, help me remember what is true. Join me in my mind and help me awaken to you. I did this only to myself. God is not the culprit. Nobody else ever did this to me. I am not affected by anyone. I chose to condemn myself to death and chose to imagine my guilt. I painted the pictures and asserted the reasons. I did this only to myself. I made up a story that I committed a sin that didn't happen! I am not guilty of a made up sin. God is not guilty and God isn't against me. God knows I am only love.

My imagined separation isn't real. My made-up exile is over. It was ridiculous to begin with. I need not keep attacking myself for something I haven't done. I need not keep pretending that a sin has really happened. I can come to my senses and see it is impossible to sin. I can reawaken and realize happily that none of this has occurred. It's just been my silly dream of isolation, where I thought myself a criminal. But nobody else was asserting for me, all along I made it up. I put this on myself and can choose once again. God is not upset with me. God doesn't believe my silly idea at all. Holy Spirit, please help me to choose differently, I want to remember my peace.

What I think I've done to myself hasn't happened. What I think I made happen did not. The sins I thought I committed never were. The causes and reasons for my needing to escape were never really there. I ran away from the scene of an imaginary crime. I don't have to run or hide. God isn't out to kill me. God is only love! I have not lost and I am not alone. Peace is restored to my mind. Separation is undone and lies are untold. It was all made up all along.

I accept the reality that sin has not occurred. I accept the truth that God always loves me. I accept that God has smiled at my silly assertion that I must be guilty. Guilt is not real and not at all serious. I've been very mistaken to believe I am guilty. Why did I take it seriously? It is not serious at all and has not happened. There is nothing to consider but God's love and peace. God's love and peace is the only truth worth knowing and I join with God right now.

I can't be sinful, I am love. I can't be guilty, I am holy. I can't be alone, God is with me. I can't be lost, I am here. I join with God in the knowing of my heart. I join with God in the light of truth. I join with

God because really there is nothing else to do. I join with God where I've always been. I open to smiling at my mistake. I open to laughing at my own silly notions. Obviously I haven't sinned! I am innocence itself, holy and beloved and pure.

My own silly lies have faded away. My own self-condemning hasn't occurred. My own self-judgement never was. My own self-pity couldn't happen. My own self-attack never got started. My own self-destruction never began. My own self-hatred had no real effect. My own self-sin is undone. I did nothing to myself, really. Nothing has happened but love. All that is real is the love of God which is here for me right now.

I join with you God and allow your love to shine. I join with you God and open to letting you love me. I join with you God to let your love be the happy truth within me. I join with you God to remember what's real and I know my illusions are impossible. I join with you God to accept who I am. I join with you God to be peaceful. I join with you God to return to joy. I join with you God to be with you.

All there is, is love and acceptance. All there is, is a heavenly welcome. All there is, is the beauty of light. All there is, is the holiness of heaven. All there is, is the glow of presence. All there is, is the love of

God. I need for nothing else and I have nothing else. I know nothing else and fear nothing else. I believe nothing else and join with nothing else. There is only God to be with and God is all there is.

Father, I am joined with you. You created me from your Self. I am your extension and your love. I am the light you created. I am always here and you are always here. We are always here together. We are one and whole, united and merged. What is you is me and is so. This is all that is and I am all that is with all that is as one. I accept and welcome everything you are. Our holiness is perfect, our peace is secure. This is the only love that's real. This is the truth and the light of my heart. I thank you and accept you and join with you now. I am home with you now and for always.

Chapter 19

I am Immortal Spirit

I am not a mortal body ready to die. I am Immortal Spirit. I am Eternal Life. I cannot end and I have not died. I am always alive and always will be.

I have never really experienced death because death is impossible. Bodies have come and gone and changed and transformed and I have been here all along. I am deathless and ageless and tireless. I have no decay in my being and no loss of life. I haven't sinned and I am not guilty. I am innocent Immortal Spirit forever.

Death is not real. Ends are just transformations, images of ends pretending to occur. Ends cannot happen because there cannot be an end to life. Life is eternal. Life in bodies, as bodies, is not life. Bodies and worlds are illusions of life. The physical universe and all other subtle universes are but shadows of living. True life is with God in divine perfection. I am divine perfection living with God in the divinity of His peace.

I cannot die. I have not been born. I have always existed and always will. Nothing can harm me or come between me and another. Nothing can stop me from being what I am. I am living an existence in God. I am unscathed by illusions of time or bodies of death. I am unchanged and unaltered by anything that seems to occur. It is not real, these illusions are not my reality. I am an example of immortality and I am Eternal Life.

Ends are pretend and continuation is real. Even in illusions there can be no real ends. Only transitions can come and go. Only changes can start and finish. Illusions change into other illusions, around and around, and none of it matters. Images of bodies may have died a trillion lifetimes and still I am wholly alive. I may have dashed myself against imaginary rocks but never did I stop my Spirit. I have transcended and traversed many illusions and yet I am at home in God. I will always be with God and will always be alive as His creation.

The illusion of the death of a body is but a projection of death away from the present. Life as a body is already death and is not real. Distance from God is the illusion of death and seems to occur every minute, every day. Every second, the body embodies the illusion of death. Every change, growth, regeneration and offspring marks an end and new beginning. Every moment represents a shift from what was to something new. Bodies and worlds are never alive and are always changing. This is not life and this is no way to live. I can live with God in eternal happiness and I allow God's life to nourish me.

I am not change, I am constant. I am not transforming, I am already myself. I am not growing, I am permanent. I am not altered, I am as I have been. I am not dead, I am alive. I am not a body, I am love. I am not adjusting, I am as God created me. I am not murdered, I am immortal.

I cannot die because I am immortal reality. I cannot end because I have no beginning. I cannot stop being who I already am. I cannot prevent myself from being real. I cannot stop God from loving me. I cannot bring an end to God's life. I cannot take away life from myself or another. I cannot change from who I am. I am the living reality of eternal life. I am truly real and truly alive. God is life and God is present. God cannot die or suffer. God is Eternal Life and I am Eternal Life with Him. I will always be eternally alive because I am the immortal Son of God.

I join with you Holy Spirit in remembering myself. I join with you and allow you to remind me of living. I join with you and allow your presence in my mind, recognizing you were already here. Please take over my thoughts of death and ideas of unreality. Please work through me to correct my mind and help me to recall my divinity. Clear my illusions and clear my dreams. Focus me on what is real. Open my heart to receive God's love and shine your love for others through me.

I am alive! I am immortal! I am eternally living and perfectly whole. Not a mark nor a tarnish nor a decay has ever touched me. I am completely flexible and fresh and new. I am loose and relaxed and joyous and playful. I am youth itself, replenished and refreshed. I am timeless and ageless and sinless and deathless. I am filled with the vitality of my Creator. I cheer at the immediate presence of life flowing through me, in me and around me, and everywhere I am. I am Immortal Spirit, death is not real and I will always be God's creation.

I cannot die because God is constantly creating me. I cannot end because God makes me forever real. I cannot stop because I cannot choose death for God. I cannot tire because God fuels my existence. I cannot suffer because flexible life runs freely through my mind. I cannot be mortal because immortality extends me. I cannot be separate because life is infinite. I cannot make fear because there is only support. I cannot lose because God is on my side. I cannot hate because I am made from love. I cannot destroy because I am so much alive. I am God's holy Son forever.

Father, take my meager dreams of death and ends and twirl them into a spiral of release. Show me how I am Immortal Spirit and open my mind to your love. Fill me with gladness at remembering what's true, and help me remember your heart. Thank you for creating me immortal and whole, and ensuring my eternal life. We will never be parted, we will never be alone, we will never be separate and we will always be one.

I am one with Love. I am one with Life. I am one with my Father forever. We are love. We are peace. We are Immortal Spirit.

Chapter 20

I am here now

I was in the past, and in the future, but I am here right now. I have always been here. I always thought I was somewhere else other than where I am, trying to find by avoiding. But here is where my heart is and here is where I am with God.

I am now. I am present. I exist eternally and beyond time. I am whole and complete in this present moment. All of time is an illusion like a movie playing on a present screen. I watch it go past from here and now. I am always in the same present moment. It is time which seems to come and go and I remain where I always am. I am still, time flows around me and I am timeless and ageless.

All of the past is gone and holds no guilt unhealed. All of the future is unbegun and holds nothing that I need. I let go of all chains and bonds holding me to what never happened. I let go of all expectations, fears and goals in imaginary futures. I transcend the past. I transcend the future. I be as God created me. I am here and now completely.

I am guiltless because nothing in the past happened. I am guiltless because I have not sinned. I have not sinned because I cannot separate from my Creator. I cannot separate from my Creator because I am with my Creator always. I am always here with my Creator and I am never lost in time. I am here right now, present and aware. Creation is timeless.

All of the nightmare that I imagined occurring was thrust through my present and locked into history. My ego thoughts used time as evidence against myself. I used my past to stop myself from being present. I used my guilt as reason to hold onto what never happened to begin with. I need not keep storing the present experience in order to retain it. There is an abundant flow of constant intelligence empowering and directing me in all ways.

I am alive in an endless boundless timeless and ageless present. I live now and am always present. I exist limitlessly and free from restrictions. I simply be where God created me. I am here with God where I've always been. I am aware of God being here with me. I open to reveal the endless present. I open to allow for love.

The past is gone and never was. The future has not happened. I have not lived in times gone by and will not live in future dreams. I am not a dream! I am not a moment in time. I am not a figure in a movie and I am not an object of time. I can only be where God created me. God created me in eternity and eternity is my home. I am home, here, now and forever in an eternal peaceful love.

Holy Spirit, correct my thinking and bring my awareness back home. Undo my wrong thinking and ambitions of avoidance. Remove the guilt that I think I should avoid. Shine toward it for me and show me it is gone. Radiate your love to reveal the complete picture. Help me to see with clarity and light that love is here and is real.

I am here! I am present! I am living this moment. I am outside of time and unbound by space. I am located in love. I am home in peace. I am present in reality. I am aware of truth. I join with my Father. I open to joy. I receive my full being. I am here.

Truth is revealed as I embrace where I am. I need not embrace an illusion. As I accept and allow and reveal what is here I transcend the images of destruction. I need not fear that I cannot accept the things which appear so awful. I do not condone them by failing to judge them, I recognize they are not there.

I release the past and release the future. I give thanks for what is now. I see that the present extends past horizons and remember my timeless nature. I am not a prisoner of time or space. I am not lost alone in the dark. I am free from my own made up guilty illusions. I am free from a past that is gone. I am free from the future and all it might bring. I am free from lifetimes and ages. I am free from all that I think they might hold. I am free to be God's creation.

I am free from time. I am free to be. I am here and I am allowed. I am open and holy and innocent and pure. I extend the presence of my Father. I flow the love that flows through me. I allow God to love and surround me. I let myself receive and extend. I give to extend what I'm given.

Peace is here. Peace is now. Peace is present. Peace is within. Peace surrounds me. Peace reassures me. Peace is my friend and my home.

Thank you Holy Spirit for what already is. Thank you for remembering truth. Thank you for knowing my innocent wholeness. Thank you for what you've undone. Thank you Father for simply being. Thank you Father for love. Thank you Father I join with you now. Thank you for creating me. I trust.

Now is. God is. I am here with God. Truth is. Love is. I am here with God. Light is. Joy is. I am here with God. Peace is. Life is. I am here with God.

Part 3

Chapter 21

I am light

I am the light of the world. I am radiance being. I am love extending love. I am the light within. I am awareness of all that is. I am the ability to see clearly. I am awake and aware in the light. I am illumination.

I thought I lived in a world of darkness where day and night seemed opposite. Yet both opposites were held apart by separation. The belief in separation between day and night is the actual darkness in action. Day is dark and night is dark because they are opposite and apart. Union and oneness are light because of the absence of separation. Light can shine and extend unhindered when obstacles of separation are gone. I am whole and unified in the light of God.

I made up darkness in my mind to try to block out the light. I invented ways to believe in darkness because I did not want to see. I wanted to avoid what I know is real so I made up walls to hide it. I shut out God with illusory darkness to stop myself being aware. But I did this to myself and even in the appearance of disempowerment I powerfully chose this to be. I am free to choose again and reclaim the awareness of light. I am in the light right now.

Light and shadows are symbols I created where shadow is made by obstruction. The obstacle to light is the problem in my mind, not the shadows it causes. I cannot fix the shadows once they're projected, I can only remove the blockages. I cannot make myself lighter than I am, I can only remember I am light. I exist already as the light of God. I am already the light of God.

The dark of night, all things black and all ways of seeming evil are just one aspect of a world of illusions. The light of day and the seemingly pleasant things are also aspects of illusions. None of them are true light and none of them are exclusive darkness. Not even images of light are light. I bought into believing that one is better, one worse, but separation is the undercurrent of judgement.

Neither images of light nor images of dark are truly representative of what light is. Light is the awareness that illusions aren't real, and that all illusions are equal. Illusions are not real in my mind at all and light is the way of my seeing. I see in light because light is whole and denies all the darkness from being.

Darkness is my attempt to block light from being. Darkness is avoidance of God. Darkness is a failure to accept what is true. Darkness is a choice for separation. Darkness is not just the image of darkness, darkness is in my perception. Darkness is the way that I look and perceive, having projected the separation.

In truth there is no darkness because there is nowhere to hide. In truth there is no darkness because light is all there is. In truth there is no darkness because God extends light forever. In truth there is no darkness because everything real is seen. I can be aware of all that exists! I can be aware of my Father. I can be aware of everything real. I can be aware of the light.

Light is real and darkness is separation. Light is true and darkness is false. Light is connection and unity and oneness. Darkness is many different things. Light is wholeness and darkness is partial. Light is immortal and darkness is death. Light is peace and darkness is turmoil. Light is sanity and darkness insane.

I can see in light because light shows me what's present. I can see in light because it reveals the whole picture. Darkness shows me frightening images because it hides the whole picture from me. Darkness destroys meaning where nothing has context and then parts of the picture seem scary. I am safe from all that is dark because light is all that there is. Light shines away the darkness and light fills my mind completely.

Holy Spirit, I join with you now, I surrender my rejection of light. I let go of resisting what is the truth and I let you show me what's real. I realize through your light that illusions are darkness and I realize I am not alone. I realize I can't see in the darkness I created and I realize I need you to help me. Please help me Holy Spirit, help me to see the light. Show me the lighted way to God's heart and help me remember His truth.

Light is here. Light is within me. Light shows me the way. Light is the sanity I have inside me. Light reveals truth all around me. Light lets me see all illusions are insane. Light shows me illusions aren't real. Light shows me the parts of the scene I was missing and helps me correct mangled meaning. In the light of truth I can see again and all I need is to see clearly. When I can see the truth in clear light I realize there's nothing to put fear in.

All I need is to see in the light, to show me that darkness is gone. All I need is to let the light shine so that shadows cannot be projected. All I need do is let shadows dissolve because infinite light has no shadow. All I need do is release my blockages to you Holy Spirit, thank you. All I need do is cease blocking the light and my dark frightening dreams will subside.

I let go of trying to stop God from shining. I let go of trying to avoid. I let go of trying to put up defenses. I let go of trying to take over. I let go of my ego insistence and resistance. I let go of trying to be separate. I let go of the darkness I imagined in my mind. I let go and allow God to shine.

I recognize with your light, Holy Spirit, that I tried to stop God's light from shining. All of my blocks were attempts to shut God out. God is the true source of light in my mind. I have not succeeded in shutting out God's love, I have not created true darkness at all. All I invented was illusion. This has been corrected, my mind is clear, and light shows me only reality.

I rejoin with God by allowing light to shine through me always. I rejoin with God by letting go of my blocks to love. I rejoin with God by allowing light to fill me. I rejoin with God my Creator. I rejoin with God because in light and in truth there is no reason to not be created. I am rejoined with God my Creator of love, where I've always existed unabated.

Death is undone and darkness is gone. Hate and fear are no more. Guilt and sadness and all forms of lies have never truly achieved anything. They were all my mistaken thinking. They were all trying to make sense of illusions. I can't find truth in a framework of darkness. I can't see the light when I'm blocking it. I let there be light and allow there be light. I let there be light to shine for me. I let there be light and allow there be light. I let there be light to shine through me.

Truth is within me where the light is shining. Truth is within me where God loves me. Truth is wholly shining in my mind. The truth is, there is no more darkness. What I thought dark was just a twisting and tangling of disjointed images. My state of insanity was simply a state of not being aware of what is.

In light and in truth, God simply is. In light there really is no attacker. In light nothing has happened to stop love from being. In light there is only God's welcome. In light all sin and guilt is forgiven. In light God is here to love me. In light there is truth

and love, joy and peace. In light I am home with my
Father.

Guilt is gone from my mind because the light is
shining. All sin is erased in the light. All
appearances of having done something wrong were
just my fragmented vision. How could I see the
peace that is true, when the light was split into
colors? I can allow the light from within to show me
the oneness of my brothers.

I am filled with light. I am filled with love. I am
filled with holy vision. I am filled with seeing all of
the truth. I am filled with complete clear awareness.
I am filled with God's presence. I'm filled with
God's love. I'm filled with His strength and His
heaven. I am filled with God's light and saved from
the dark. I am filled with God's light-filled
abundance.

I live only in the light. I am only in the light. I be
only in light. I am light! The light that fills me and
the light that surrounds me extend me as light from
light. This light is all there is to see. This light is the
love of God. This light is my home and my loving
safe-haven. This light is my real true nature. This
light is heaven. This light is me. In this light I am
light forever. I am the light. God is the light. We are
all the light together.

Chapter 22

I am not a separate self

My mind is joined with others. I am never alone. My thoughts are shared with others. None of my thoughts are my own. My perception encompasses others. I never see only myself. My healing also heals others. My healing heals all as One.

I am not a separate being with a separate mind and a separate identity. I am one with God. I made up this small self to pretend to be something I'm not. I made up bodies and lifetimes to identify with but they are not my identity. I identified with images in a movie and thought they are who I am. But I cannot be a passing image, at the whim of a script all through time. I am united with my Father and love is who I am.

My body is just an image. My body is not my Self. I cannot be a body lest I die when the body ends its seeming life. I project the body from my mind. The body is inside my dream. I cannot be further inside the body when the body is inside of me. This body is not my identity. This body is not who I am. I am not a body, I am Immortal Spirit. I am not an image of a self, or a self image, or a self-made identity. I am only as God created me to be and I am God's holy Son.

My belief in being a separate self was my attempt to forget my True Self. My attempt to be a multitude of bodies was my attempt to not be what I am. I wanted to hide my True Identity so that I could pretend to be something else. I wanted to be something else so that I could explore being separate and alone. But separate bodies cannot house my nature, for I am Infinite Spirit. No body can encompass my Infinite Self.

This body seems to wrap around a fragment of my mind as if to say, I am inside it. This body is a solidification of my idea of being separate. My belief in being this body is no different from my belief that other people are also bodies. Either we are all bodies or none of us are bodies. None of us are bodies at all. Our bodies cannot keep us separate. Our minds cannot be kept apart. The seeming abrupt ending of the body's perimeter cannot keep us from the oneness we are. We are all one in God.

Not only am I not a separate single body, but I am also not many or few. Other people's bodies are not who they are any more than I am a body. None of us can exist as separate identities, lest we all live in separate worlds. All of our fantasies of unique will and thought are isolations of mind acting separate. How can minds be joined when minds are separated by bodies? How can the Son of God be whole and complete when split into billions of pieces? We are not split, we are whole and complete and our bodies are not real at all.

I identified with illusions of specialness so that I could be separate from God. I thought the illusions I made were real to me and then thought they were who I am. My investment in them to make them appear was my choice to believe that I am them. I formed these illusions from my own self and so it follows I must be what they are. And so I thought I had become illusions of difference, separate selves and countless variations. But this is not who I am. I am one complete whole Son of God and this is all God created.

Holy Spirit, clearly I am mistaken about who I am. I've forgotten my True Nature. Please take over and shine your light to fill my mind with the truth. Help me remember who I am. Help me know myself. Help me let go of the illusion that I am embodied.

Undo the blocks I've put in place to prevent me from being myself.

I am immortal. I am one Self. I am as God created me. I cannot be anything else. I am immortal and I am free. I am free of the self that is little and pretend. I am free of the identity I invented. I am free from restriction to bodies and death. I am free to be as I truly am. I am free to join with my own Self again. I am free to remember my being. I am free to look upon myself as complete. I am free from illusions of separation. I am holy, I am pure, I am innocent and one. God created me to be an extension of love and love is all I can be.

I am not a body, I am free. I am not identified with a body, I am identified with Holy Spirit. I can take the Holy Spirit's hand and let go of the ego's hand. I don't have to take a frightening leap, I can simply exchange lies for the truth. I hold your hand Holy Spirit, take my hand safely and don't let me go. Help me to feel the strength of your certainty and know the conviction of True Self. This separate person who I thought I was is not who I am at all. I am much more expansive. I am much more open. This separate person self doesn't have to die or be lost or cut off from my life. I can simply become aware that I am more than this. I am more than a separate being. I include the love of my Father.

Holy Spirit, show me myself. Let me see who I am. Reveal the truth that is hiding inside me. Awaken my mind once again. I am Spirit. I am truth. I am living immortal life. I am whole. I am forgiven. I am free from all forms. I am joined. I am unified. I am one. I am love. I am one with you Holy Spirit. I am one with my Self.

I am at peace because I am who I really am. I am at peace because nothing in form applies to me. I am at peace because the world doesn't touch who I am. I am at peace because I am free from illusion. I am at peace because God has created me peaceful. I am at peace because my heart is healed. I am at peace because dreams cannot hurt who I am. I am at peace because God's love is real.

I don't have to try to be something I'm not. I don't have to become something else. I don't have to fix or change or repair. I don't have to solve the world's problems. I don't have to slave to achieve pointless goals. I don't have to provide any answers. I don't have to figure out what the world means. I don't have to worry about a body. I don't have to isolate in order to be safe. I don't have to fear for my safety. I don't have to worry that I might not exist. I don't have to wait for my death. I am utterly immortal and utterly free of the tyranny of separate identity. I can join God in peace and be as I am, I can be as God created me.

I release this separate self and let it be. I don't have to try to change it. I've identified with countless separate selves. None of them are who I am. These separate identities do not have the capacity to change into who I am really am. They are all tiny personalities formed from images and illusions of identity. Images cannot change to represent God. Images cannot become who I am. Why would I need an image of myself if the image were an accurate representation? I can throw images aside and let go of the fear that letting go of self would mean death. I am alive in God and always will be. I am alive because God created me.

My only fear is that letting go of ego will mean I will no longer exist. But this is only because I've identified myself with the thing that has never existed. If it ends and if I am it, then I would end along with it. And the ego is clear in making it known it intends for me to hold onto it always. So how can I let go of being a small self when it would mean the end of my being? I don't have to worry, it's just a diversion. Holy Spirit has a solution.

I need only remember my True Self is real. I need only take hold of Love's hand. I need only hold on to the strength of the light and remember I'm always eternal. All I need do is let go of identifying with an ego that wasn't there all along. I only need give up my continued dependence on a body that isn't myself. I can shift my identity to my Higher Self. I can shift my identity to Love. I can shift my identity to something other than ego. I can shift my identity from the body. I can shift my identity to the Truth that I am. I can shift and remember the Truth. I can easily remember I am love, I am light. I can trust Holy Spirit to help me.

As I release my grip on the world, I release my grip on the ego. As I release my grip on separation, I release my grip on all dying. As I release my grip on fear, I release my grip on destruction. As I release my grip on death, I release my grip on illusion. It's safe for me to let go my grip. It's safe for me to trust Holy Spirit. It's safe for me to allow Him to help me. It's safe for me to change identity. I can change my identity back to who I am. I can change my identity from illusions. I can change my identity from being a body. I can return to who I already am.

My True Self is always here. My True Self is my true nature. My True Self is God's creation. My True Self is love. My True Self is filled with God's protection. My True Self is secure and safe. My True Self doesn't switch and change. My True Self is always present. I don't have to make my True Self what it is. My True Self is already established. My True Self was put in place by God's love. My True Self is permanently real. My True Self is higher my True Self is lighter my True Self is filled with joy. My True Self is peaceful my True Self is loving my True Self is beyond being destroyed.

My True Identity is God's holy Son. My True Identity is here. My True Identity is not in illusions. My True Identity is real. I already am my True Self! I already am free from ego. I already am much more than a body. I already am Infinite Spirit. Everyone else is already True Self. Everyone is free from ego. Everyone else is much more than a body. Everyone is Infinite Spirit. We are all the True Self that God has created. We are all one True Self in Spirit. We all share the Identity that we are all One. We are all the One Son God created.

I share in True Self with All That Is. I share in True Self with everyone. I share in True Self with God my Father. I share in True Self with Love. I open and share everything I am. I open and share God's extension. I open and share the love that I am. I open to allowing God's nature. I am created after God and modeled on His being. I am made from what God is made of. I am His creation and create as He does. I am the perfection of His creation. I am just like God in every way. I am holy, innocent and joyful. I am at peace in the same way that God is at peace. I am at peace knowing I'm with Him.

Father, I am home with you. I am here with you. I am love. Father I am filled with you. I am love with you. I am your creation. I extend your love. I express your love. I extend your love around me. I spread your love and see your love and recognize your love as myself. I am your love. I am your peace. I am your eternal creation. I am your Son. I am your Son. I am your Son for always.

I am with you in peace, I am with you in love, and Love is who I am.

Chapter 23

I am healthy

I am not sick, I am filled with health. I am healthy because God created me free from all problems. I haven't become ill and I am not diseased. I have never fallen ill and never will. My mind is free from illness and sickness. My mind is free to be healthy.

I chose countless ailments and forms of disagreement. I chose not to love myself and to let myself be vulnerable. I chose to believe I could suffer in countless ways. I chose to allow myself to appear to be at the effect of a body, at the effect of a world. But I am not a body, I am Holy Spirit and I cannot create real sickness. I can only invent illusions of sickness which I project out as this body. Yet my mind is healed and whole and I am cured from the nightmare of defectiveness.

My guilt about pushing God away only created disease. I was not at ease with myself. My guilt about trying to destroy love produced states of attack upon myself. I thought I deserved to be punished and so I punished myself. My guilt projected as form and all form is a form of dis-ease. Whether my body seems sick or healthy, it is neither. My body is not the source of health. My body is not the source of sickness. I am truly healthy because I am not a body and I am not guilty of sin.

My body has no sickness of its own. My body cannot cause me sickness. My body is not sick or suffering. The problem is not with my body. The problem is not in my body. The problem is in my mind. The problem is my misperception of God. I seem to experience sickness in my body but my body is not the sickness. My mind believes in sickness and experiences this belief as suffering. I am only sick with the belief in sickness and this belief is now undone. Only my mind can conceive of sickness and only my mind can be corrected. My mind is free from issues of unhealth and I am free to be healthy again.

I haven't destroyed love and I haven't destroyed God. I haven't caused bad things to happen. I haven't managed to be separate and alone. I haven't succeeded in sinning. I haven't travelled far from home. I haven't shut out God's being. I haven't managed to create a world where only suffering is real. I haven't been able to hate myself into a body. I haven't achieved my own self-destruction. I haven't inflicted lies. I am pure and holy as God created me and always will be healthy.

I performed all sickness upon myself. I sickened myself deliberately. I chose all sickness and made it all up. All sickness is my mental illusion. I invented all disease with my thoughts of separation. I conceived of all weakness, frailty and death. I made myself my own victim. Nobody did this for me or to me. Nobody caused me to suffer. Nothing happened to create this. I am clearly mistaken in thinking I am guilty and that I need to suffer in sickness. I am not sick of God and I am not sick of my Self. I am not truly sick at all. This is just an illusion. I am whole and healed in God and all sickness is gone.

Holy Spirit, please take my hand and lighten my perspective. Show me the immaculate state of mind in which I have no ailment. Help me be aware of the truth that I am not sick. Help me to see that I am neither a healthy body nor a diseased body. Help me remember that all bodies are illusion and only my mind is pure. Release my thinking from tangled thoughts of desperate means and measures.

I am healed from sickness! It is undone. It hasn't happened. It never was. Sickness hasn't happened.

Sickness isn't real. All disease is imagined and pretend. None of it is real. I have never been sick and I cannot be sick. I am not sick at all. My mind is healed and whole and complete. My mind is not sickened at something I didn't do. I have not killed God, I have not separated, I have not lost my mind. I am healed and whole and holy and complete. I am shining in the love of my Father.

My mind is healthy, my mind is whole, my mind is still as it was created. My mind is cleansed of all illusions. My mind is free from disruption. My mind is spotless. My mind is clean. My mind is holy and immortal. There never has been a sickness in my mind. There never has been anything but love. Love is here and love is clear and love has cleared my mind. All of my beliefs that I could ever be sick were always mistaken and blind.

My body has never been sick, I was just imagining. Other people's bodies have never been sick, I was just imagining. All sickness and all disease and even death are gone because there are no real bodies at all. All disease and all loss has been forever undone. Death is no more. Disease hasn't happened. Sickness is unreal. Upset is not here. There is no sickness. There is no guilt. There is no sin. There is no death. There is only health. There is only love. There is only the life of God.

I am the health within me. I am completely recovered. All effects of unreal causes have been completely undone. There have been no consequences from imagined separation. Nothing real has come from it. It simply hasn't happened and I am unchanged. I haven't become sick. I haven't stopped being healthy. I haven't stopped being love. I haven't stopped being God's creation. I have only continued as love.

Love flows through me. Life flows through me. I am recharged with the fuel of love. God's living force creates my well being. God Himself does love me! I am an extension of living health. I am the output of life. I am a channel of holy healing. I am a funnel for love. I reveal true health wherever I go. I am an example of wellbeing. The peace in my mind extends and expands. The light in me is forgiving.

Holy Father, extend your love. Flow your love through me now. Help me to allow you to wash away my belief in a sickness that I cannot be. Open my mind to allow in your love, open my heart to your heart. Continue extending me as your creation, as a shining example of love. I am immaculate and unchanged and healthy in your sight. I am completely as you created me. I have not altered or adjusted or failed. I am always a blessing of wholeness.

I am the love. I am the light. I am the peace. I surrender to love. I allow my true health. I flow God's love. I accept the truth that I am healed. I accept I have never been sick. I accept I am not a body. I am Immortal Spirit filled with love's truth. Death and disease cannot touch me. I am immortal and immune and unable to die. I cannot be lost or alone. I was always pretending I could ever be less than I am. I am completely filled with God's love. I am here in love forever.

I am healthy. I am alive. I am healed and whole. Thank you, Father for already establishing complete total freedom. I am free from disease. I am free from death. Death and disease are unreal. I am holy. I am God's Son. I am fully the love that's within me. I am light. I am healed. I am peace. I am joy. I am happy. I am one. I am free.

Chapter 24

I am forgiven

All that I ever thought wrong is undone. All that I ever thought happened did not. All that I ever felt guilty for I am innocent. All that I ever saw as evil is not there. All that I thought was lost is now found. All that I thought was a sin is not so. All that I am is forgiven. All that I am is love.

I am forgiven of the thought that I am justified in being punished for a guilty sin I did not commit. The sin has not occurred. Nothing has gone wrong. There has been no effect. The error is not real. I am not guilty and deserve no punishment. I am forgiven because I have not sinned. I am forgiven of the thought that I committed a crime against God, truth and myself. This crime has not occurred and cannot occur. I am not guilty of a crime that is impossible. I am forgiven because I have not committed a sin against God. I am forgiven because I am holy.

God's role is not to forgive me nor to judge me with punishment. God has not condemned me nor sees me as guilty. God does not recognize or acknowledge or agree with my own belief in my own sinfulness. God is not aware of sin because there is no sin. God is sane and knows the reality of His infinite Self. My belief that I have sinned, or that I am guilty and should be afraid of punishment, is my own error. My error can be corrected because it is not real. My error has already been corrected because it has not happened. I need merely become aware that I am already innocent.

I cannot be guilty because I am created innocent. I am created from innocence and cannot become guilty. I can only remain as God created me as sinless, guiltless and fearless. I am forgiven of all my mis-beliefs about God. I am forgiven of my error in thinking. I am forgiven of the thoughts that I am separate. None of these errors are true and none of them are permanent or real. All of these errors are mistaken perceptions and all of them are corrected. I open to accept that all of my mistaken beliefs have not happened, have had no consequences, and are not real. I am free to be innocent as God created me forever.

I believed in sin because I wanted to believe I could actually separate from God. It is impossible to separate from God because God is everywhere. I believed in guilt because I thought I really had sinned and wanted to make sin permanent. I used guilt to lock sin in place and to shift to focussing on judgement. But I cannot be guilty because separation is impossible and has not happened. If separation is impossible, sin is impossible. If sin is impossible, guilt is impossible. I cannot be guilty because I cannot be sinful. I cannot be sinful because I cannot be separate from God. I am unified with God in complete and permanent wholeness.

I thought that because impossible sin had occurred, and impossible guilt could come from it, that I could be impossibly afraid of impossible punishment. I believed in fear of punishment so that I could lock my guilt away and shift my focus to punishment. I wanted to believe in punishment so that I could keep guilt intact. I wanted to be afraid so that I could run away from guilt. I used fear as a protection in attempting to avoid punishment and to keep it in place. But I need not be afraid because fear is not real. Fear is undone and does not exist. Fear is impossible because guilt is impossible. Guilt is impossible because sin is impossible. Sin is impossible because separation is impossible. Separation is impossible because love is infinitely real.

As a result of fear I could not live with myself. I fled into the recesses of my mind. I escaped into illusions and dreams of worlds that don't exist. I tried to hide from fear to keep it in place. To push fear away and to keep it intact I projected it outward as a universe. I put myself into many bodies to further disguise my identity. And finally I laid my own bodies to rest once certain punishment of death had transpired.

Either way, avoiding God or not, I made sure to believe I should die. I make sure that death would be my end and that death is the end of God. But it is impossible to be dead because God does not punish. It is impossible to fear because God does not punish. It is impossible to be guilty because God does not punish. It is impossible to be sinful because God does not punish. I am Immortal Spirit, holy and innocent and only love is real.

Holy Spirit, light of truth in my mind and heart, I join with you now to reunite with myself. Please take over the reigns of my sanity and clear away the illusions of death. Help me to see with your true vision the truth as God created it. I am truly forgiven for all of the above.

I am truly forgiven of death. I am forgiven of the lies and the dreams of separation. I am forgiven of being a body. I am forgiven of believing in separation. I am forgiven of every behavior. I am forgiven of all that I think I have done. I am forgiven of every mistake. I am completely forgiven.

Absolutely everything that I ever thought I did to produce a real effect on myself or another has not happened. I am forgiven because none of it occurred at all. Absolutely everything that I ever believed about myself being other than God's holy innocent Son was a mistake. It is impossible that I be other than God's holy innocent Son. I am holy and innocent because God created me holy and innocent. Absolutely every crime, every error, every upset, every mis-step, every judgement, every revenge, every murder, every tear, every playful experience in illusions, every dream and every death has all been forgiven and released because it has not happened. I let it go and allow it to not be.

I look with light toward the world of fear and see it is not there. I look with light toward the dream of guilt and see it is not justified. I look with light toward the illusion of sin and see there is none there. I look with light toward the idea of separation and see it is not real. I look with light at myself and recognize that without these illusions I am unchanged. I look with light and see myself as I am, in truth, in light, in Spirit.

I am the living light and the deep love that is God's being. God does not hold anything against me. God does not find me guilty. God does not think I've done something wrong. God is not going to punish me. God is simply going to laugh at my insistence that anything wrong is real. God just wants to love me and does. God just knows I am love. God shares His peace with me. God shares all His love with me. God smiles and reminds me I'm home.

I am forgiven. It is undone. I have not sinned. I am not guilty. I am unafraid. I have no reason to be dead. I see only truth. I see only light. All is forgiven and there is only peace. All is forgiven and there is only love. All is forgiven and there is only laughter. All is forgiven and there is only God. I am with you Father, here and now, in the light of truth forever. I join with you. I open to allow your love in. Thank you for reminding me that only love is real. Thank you for extending love through me. I am your love. I am your Son. I am your Holy Spirit. All is forgiven and all is undone. I open my eyes and I see it. I am created from your beautiful love. All I can do is to be it.

Chapter 25

I am like God

I am created after my Father. I am like Him in every way. I am not something else. I am not different. I am only in the likeness of my Creator, as I've always been. I cannot be other than He is. I am an extension of His love. I am His One Son.

I am not separate or distinguished from my Father. I am created after His likeness and reflect His being. I thought I could be something else and set off on a journey of imagined difference. The journey led me to the ultimate difference: death. I met with non-existence because the journey had not begun. I am only with God in God's mind and I am created by His extension.

I thought myself different by identifying with form and error. I thought I was a universe, a body, an organism, but I am light. I identified with the dreams I imagined and pretended to be what cannot be created. Without God's sustaining presence all of these forms weren't real. I could only find death without the loving presence of my Father's love. Yet I am free from death because I am created from life.

My body is not who I am any more than I am a small separate part of a dream. My separate self is not who I am any more than I am a small separate part of totality. I am not broken apart nor fragmented into pieces. I am only my original True Self basking in the endless light of my Creator. I am God's Son, holy and innocent for an eternity.

Dear Holy Spirit in my mind, thank you for being the reminder of my eternal originality as God's creation. Thank you for shining light on my true nature so that I can be aware of who I am. Please take my hand and lift me above the illusions of difference in me. Lift me up from the nightmare of dreams ending always in death and disaster. Remind me of what is true and what is real. Remind me of who I am.

God created me. I am His Son. I am created from His being. His nature is love. Since I am created from His being I must be made from love. Since I am like Him, I must be love also. I cannot be made from anything else. I am only made from love. I am love, just like my Father, because He created me from love, with love. I am like my Father and we are Love as one.

God is truth and God created me, so I must be truth also. I am incapable of being false or fake because I am created by truth. I am made of truth, I come from truth and I can only be truth. I cannot be a lie, I cannot be a sin, I cannot be an evil dream. I can only be truth because I am like my Creator. My Creator is truth and therefore I am truth also. I can only be the truth that is true of my Creator for I am like Him. God and I are Truth as one.

God is life and God created me so I must be life also. I must be incapable of death because I am only made from life. I cannot turn into death because God did not create death. God only created me as His Living Son and I can only be alive. I am life itself because I am extension of life. I extend God's life forever. I am His United Living Son and always will be alive in Him. I am like God because I am His Son and we both are alive as one.

God is whole and God created me so I am whole also. I cannot be incomplete because God shares everything with me. God is wholeness and not separation. I come from God and God creates me from wholeness. I must therefore be whole because I cannot be anything else. I am like God so I am whole just like Him. I share everything wholly and completely because I am in the wholeness of my Father.

God is peace, calm and sure. God is safe from illusions. I am created from God's total peace and I am extended from His peace forever. Therefore I cannot be upset or endangered or troubled or threatened. I can only be the peace He created. I can only be like my Father. My Father is peaceful and therefore I am peaceful with Him. I can only be the peace of mind that extends the peace of God. I am only peace because I am like my Father and He is always peaceful.

God is light, with nothing to hide. God is radiant total awareness. God is aware of all that is and His openness and awareness are light. God created me within His light and holds me within His light. I am an extension of light and awareness. I am just like His light. I am the light that He extends. I am the light He is made of. I am created from a living light and I cannot be made from darkness. There is nowhere that my light cannot shine. I am always the light that is shining.

God is joy because there is no reason not to be. God is joyful because nothing is against Him. Only joy is present in God and I am created by God. I am just like Him and so I must be joyful also. I cannot be unhappy or filled with despair because God did not put despair in me. I can only be joyful always and forever. I can only be the joy of God. God is joyful that I am created as an extension of His total joy. I am eternally filled with joy because God is joyful always.

God is love. God is complete total love. God is welcoming and God is accepting and God loves me fully forever. God created me from love. God created me with love. God created me and extended me from love. God made me with love. I am created by love, I am only love, I am love itself in God. God holds me in His heart with love. I am in His heart forever. I can only be love. I cannot be hate, or fear, or murder or death. I cannot be sin or guilt or punishment, I can only be the love that He is. I am like God and God is love so I am love like Him. I can only be love because God is love and God created me with love.

Father, I accept I am like you. I open to your love. I accept I cannot be anything you didn't create. I am simply just like you. I did not create you but you created me. I am the extension of your being. All of your properties I inherit completely. All of your nature is my truth. I am suspended in an extension of your love. I am entirely created by you. I am completely filled with your love. I am only as you created me.

If you are love, then I am love. If you are peace, then I am peace. If you are light, then I am light. If you are joy, then I am joy. If you are truth, then I am truth. If you are real, then I am real. If you are everywhere, then I am everywhere. If you are open, then I am open. If you are safe, then I am safe. If you are awake, then I am awake. If you are one, then I am one. I am one with you.

I am only like God, I am nothing else. I am only the love that He is. I have no other identity. I am only His Son. I am just like my Father's love. I have nothing else. I need nothing else. I am nothing else at all. I allow myself to only be the love extending from my Father. I be the love. I live the love. I extend the love. I feel the love. I allow the love. I have only love. I can only be love because God is.

I am love, just like my Father. I am just like God. I am love. I am only love. I am love forever.

Chapter 26

I am peaceful

Every dream has stopped. All dreams have ended. There is no sound. There are no images. Everything is calm. Nothing is moving. There is no change. There is no threat. Problems have dissolved. Nothing has occurred. Peace is all there is.

I created conflict within myself and have only experienced it there. I upset myself with a fear and fright I invented. I made up a dream of a world of hate. I made up a universe of pain. I wrote all of history, time and space. I built imagined stories that came and went. All of it has passed and is no more. None of it is here. I am safe from fear and safe from illusion. Peace is all there is.

I am calm in my centerless being. I am peaceful everywhere. I am open to knowing there is no need to worry. I feel the freedom from insanity. All my worries have ended. All my fears have gone. All my nightmare dreams never were. All my being is one. I am calm and at peace. I am quiet and still. Nothing is happening but love. I relax and let go. I be still and quiet. I let myself be with God.

Guilt is over. Sin is undone. Death is cancelled. Fear is unreal. I melt into a deep inner abiding. I let myself by here. I need do nothing. I need not escape. I have no more need to run. There's nothing to run from and nowhere to hide. Nothing is chasing me down. Fear has stopped. Ego has ended. Peace has swept over me. I quietly be with my Father's love. I join in peace completely.

There are no noises. There is no alarm. There is nothing troubling me. Inner pain has completely dissolved. Light and truth fill and surround me. I am fully here. I am clear of dreams. Peace and stillness dwell in me. A gentle glow of love flows through me. I have no boundaries to contain it. I am so open I have no limits. I expand to fill to infinity. My Being has no edges. My Being is unlimited. My being is one with God.

I am safe completely. I am safe in love. I am safe from everything scary. There are no dreams here. There is only love here. It has always been this calm. God is with me. God is around me. I recognize and remember Him. I know you, Father. I know who you are. I know who I am as I know you. I see your being. I see your light. I see your welcome and love. I rest reassured. I rest and relax. I can be with you now and be happy.

I trust you Father to keep me with you. I trust you to love me completely. I trust you to hold me in your perfect light. I trust you to take complete care of me. I trust you because you welcome me completely. I trust you because you are love. I trust you because I have nothing to fear. I trust in your love completely. I am peaceful with you. I am safe with you. I have no more reason to doubt. I am here with you. I am one with you. I cannot be without.

I let you take care of me Father. I let you love me now. I let you know what is best for me. I let you look after my Self. I let you show me. I let you direct me. I make no decision of my own. I need no decision to accept that you love me. I let you love me. I am home. I am in your love. I am here, I am here with you. I am happy to be with you. I am happy in love. I am happy you have everything taken care of.

I need not fear. I can joyfully love. I can cheer that you love me completely. I am happy to love. I am joyful to be love. I am filled with love again. I am love with you. I am light with you. I am peace with you forever. You are my friend. You are my Creator. I am restored again.

This is a happy day. Now I remember God's joy. Now that I know that God is all there is, I can rejoice and be happy and laugh. There is only God! God is real! God is happiness and light! I can dance in God's love. I am new in His love. I am peaceful because love is real. I am a piece of love. I am all of love. I extend God's love. I am love! I celebrate being the love that is here. I accept I am loved completely.

Now there is peace I can let go and play. Now there is peace I am happy. Now there is peace I have no concern. Now there is peace I can stay. Now there is peace I am safe and secure. Now there is peace I am relieved. Now there is peace I am light truth and love. Now I know peace is here with me.

Thank you Father for sharing your peace. I am peaceful and happy with you. I let you, allow you, accept you and join you. I am peaceful with you in your love. I'm happy with you. I'm safe with you. I join with you in peace. I love with you. I joy with you. I be with you completely.

Chapter 27

I am holy

There is not a thing I've done nor a thing I've seen that can take away my holiness. I am holy because I am innocent in God's eyes. God's light shines on me with complete open radiance, showering me with perfect love. I can be and do nothing else but absorb and reflect God's love shining through me. I am holy in His sight and always will be. I am holy as God's One Son.

My aims to be less than holy have always led to failure. I used loss, separation, death and destruction to try to stop myself from being holy. But by using failure as a tool I could only fail to stop myself from being what I am. Using powerlessness as a tool I could only lack the power to stop myself being what I am. Using death as a tool my attempt to stop myself from being what I am ended before it could begin. I have utterly failed to stop myself from being what I am. I am holy and innocent and all is forgiven and released.

My holiness is an extension of God's holiness. My wholeness is an extension of God's wholeness. I am holy because I am pure. I am holy because I am innocent. I am holy because God's love for me is sacred and true. I cannot be anything else but holy. God created me from His holiness, from His wholeness, and as a whole. I am wholly holy because I am God's creation. I am wholly created and holy created. I am wholeness and holiness itself. What else could I be when God shines a light so bright all I can do is be? I am God's holy creation, now and forever. I am God's whole holy Son.

I thought I was attacking God but my attempts to attack were withdrawals. I thought I was exploding God but my attempts to explode were implosions. I thought I was lurching toward God with deathly intent but my lurches were always retreat. I thought I was stopping God by encasing Him within my limits but my limiting confined only myself. Every time I screamed at God my screams were void of presence. Whenever I thought I was increasing my size, my size was only decreasing. Every attempt I ever made to destroy God failed because everything I think I do to another is only done to myself. I have completely failed to harm or change God in any way and have only seemed to harm myself. Yet I am unharmed because even my self-harm is impossible. I am harmless because I cannot be harmed. I am harmless because I am holy. In my holy harmlessness and I cannot harm or be harmed.

My efforts to push God away, to create separation, only pushed myself away from God. My efforts to make it seem that God has abandoned me only made myself lonelier. My efforts to blame God for causing me to sin only caused me to believe in sin. My attempt to make God guilty for what He has not done only made me believe in guilt. God is immortal! I cannot harm God or change God or deter God from being as He is. I cannot and have not taken away His purity, His love, His light, His laugh or His holiness. God is unchanged in His knowing and creation of what I am. I am nothing else but God's holy Son forever.

My friend Holy Spirit, I recognize you are with me and have been always. I recognize you are always here and it is me that seems to go away. I recognize you are with me even when I think you have left me alone. It is my own foolish ways that convince myself I'm suffering in isolation. All I need do is open to the awareness of your loving presence. You are here and I am with you. It is not up to you to reveal yourself to me, but up to me to accept you are revealed. You are not hiding from me, you are not escaping from me, you are not attacking me at all. I trust you and acknowledge you and put my mind into your hands. Please take over my thoughts of separation and shine your light on my belief in illusion. Help me to see with your clarity the truth that is already here.

I am holy and innocent. I am love. I am already pure within myself. I haven't done anything wrong. I haven't hurt God at all. God obviously loves me greatly. God creates me with His love! I am here in the light that has always been here. I am clear in the light that has always been clear. I am peace itself, everywhere and everywhen. I am alive in the truth that shines within. I am already released from the illusions of separation that I made myself. I am already holy and light. I am already home with my Father. I am already here in love.

Pieces of my Self are not missing. I am already holy and wholly complete. Parts of my mind are not hidden. I am already holy and wholly complete. Aspects of my awareness are not concealed. I am already holy and wholly complete. Chunks of my Self have not been lost. I am already holy and wholly complete. Sparks of my identity have not separated off. I am already holy and wholly complete. God loves me! I am the love that God

loves me with. There is no separate me to love - I am
the love itself. I am God's love. God is love and I am
one with God.

My attempt to separate from God has not worked. I
am not separate from God at all. My attempt to
harm God or change God's behavior has not
worked. I have not changed God at all. My struggle
to identify myself as a body has not worked. I am
not a body at all. My effort to isolate myself from
God and everyone has not worked. I can never be
alone while God is always with me. My ambition to
take over as God's replacement and to see the end of
God existing has not worked. Thankfully God is
immortal and immune and is permanently present
forever. My chore of constantly pushing God away
has not worked. God hasn't moved an inch and
loves me deeply, intimately and everlasting. I have
achieved nothing beside being as God intended. I
have failed to make failure successful. I can only be
as God intended. I am wholly with God forever.

I exist in eternity where God dwells. I exist as the
extension of love. I exist as a oneness that extends
forever. I exist in a luminous light. I exist beyond all
bodies, space and time. I exist in Spirit immortal. I
exist as peace, joy and abundance. I exist as God's
holy Son. I exist as myself as God created me. I exist

as an endless being. I exist with no limits. I exist without end. I exist in the love of God.

Father, thank you for showing me eternal love. Thank you for your radiant peace. Thank you for always being as you are. Thank you for creating me with you. Thank you for the oneness which merges us together. Thank you for our happy home. Thank you for ensuring immortality forever. Thank you for loving as one.

I am holy and peaceful. I am holy and innocent. I am holy and whole as your Son.

Chapter 28

I am not guilty

I thought I was guilty but I am not. God loves me. I thought I sinned but I did not. God loves me. I thought I should be afraid because I am guilty, but I am fearless. God loves me. Anything I thought I did or I thought happened has not happened and I am not guilty. I am guiltless and sinless, holy and innocent and always am only this.

I thought that many things really happened. I was mistaken. I thought that since they happened they could not be undone. Who can undo time? I made it seem that once something occurred it could never be undone, changed or corrected. I assembled an earthly reality to paint a picture of time and space. In my picture I suggested that separation is occurring, and then relegated those events to the past. I took the appearance of separation and turned it into an irreversible sin, locked away as history. But I was mistaken and I forgot that I made this all up. The past is not a holding place for a sin that has not happened. I have not sinned and I am not guilty. I am holy and innocent always.

Because of the things which seemed to occur outside of my doing, it seemed the only way to allow such sins to be pardoned was to let someone else off the hook. I thought if I could bestow a pardon on my projected source of sin, I could exercise my throne of ego power to give a pardon of sin where it was not deserved. I saw myself as a savior of those who cannot save themselves, having determined they are all sinners and having condemned them to death. If they are the ones who have sinned then I must be the one who has every right to judge them, negatively or positively. But my positive pardons are no different from my negative judgements, both of them making sin real, having projected it outward. Nobody else is the cause of sin and I am not the cause of sin either. Sin is not real and has not happened at all.

I find others guilty because I want to hold sin against them. I put my own belief in sin onto them so that I can seem to escape its punishment. I project my guilt onto others so that I can find them unworthy and not myself. But I am deluding myself. I have already decided I am guilty and sinful. I have already decided I am unworthy of forgiveness. I have already decided my separation from God is permanent. I have already decided to believe in my own death. But death is unreal and I am eternally innocent.

I put all of these beliefs onto seeming others so that they can carry the weight of them for me. But they are unable to carry a weight not their own and I never really escape it. I'm still carrying the weight of guilt even if I pretend to disown it. I am the one who thinks I am guilty. I decided this all by myself. I disown the guilt and project it out but it does not go away. Deep down I still believe it. It is still a part of my experience whether inside myself or outside. I can't escape from sin by blaming others for my own self hatred. In truth, neither I nor others have done anything wrong at all.

My initial belief that I am sinful is in fact a mistake. I can't be sinful because God created me innocent and I am incapable of actually sinning. The sin is not outside of me, it's a false belief in my own mind. The guilt that surrounds it and stems from it is not outside of me, it's a false belief in my own mind. The fear that follows the guilt is not outside of me, it's a false belief in my own mind. Where did this belief come from, and who has the power to save me? I am saved because it is not really there at all.

Holy Spirit, light my way. Illuminate my imagined deception. Reveal to me true perception so that I may see this sin is not real. Help me to look at who created this and help me to undo my belief in it. If it truly has not happened to me, then help me to see this is so.

I can't be sinful because I am holy. Holiness is always holy. I can't be a perpetrator because there is nothing separate to attack. I can't attack God because His life is immortal. I can't change who I am because I can't alter God's creation. I have nothing to fear because I am not guilty. I need not be guilty because I haven't sinned. I haven't sinned because separating from God is impossible. I can't separate from God because God knows only unity. I am unified in God and free from sin forever.

I made up the insistence that I am guilty and condemned. I made it appear that someone else outside of me did this to me. I blamed God for my perceived error and tried to believe He has judged me. I already believed God had sentenced me to exile, punishment and death. I already believed I am in hell. I already tried to convince myself that I no longer had the power to undo this. I am waiting for someone to rescue me. I am waiting for a separate self to change their judgement of me because I give them power to change me. I've accepted that someone out there found me guilty, because of what I did to them and God. But there is nobody else out there to judge me. There is nobody separate to decide I am guilty. Nobody else has the power to decide that I am not God's Son. Even I cannot make myself something I am not. Even I have no power to undo love. I can only accept what I am within. I can only be God's holy Son.

No-one else is guilty of a crime I didn't commit. No-one else is sinful for doing what I have not done. No-one else need be afraid of a punishment that is not deserved of me. No-one else need die as a result of a crime that I have not accomplished. Nobody else has caused me to separate. Nobody else has judged me. Nobody else has decided my fate. Nobody else has condemned me. I made this myself, I created the lie, I imagined my guilt in separation. I invented the sin in my own mind and imagined it's really real. Yet it has not happened at all! I am totally mistaken to think it has. I simply am incapable of separating from love. I can only be God's holy Son as He created me to be. I am God's guiltless Son forever.

Nobody else is deciding my demise. Nobody else has power over me. Nobody else can determine my future. Nobody else can condemn me. Nobody else has taken power from me. Nobody else has decided

I'm guilty. Nobody else has ever put this onto me. Nobody else is doing this for me. I have made up my own imagined guilt. I have made up my own imagined judgement. I have made up my own state of sin and guilt. I have made up my own undeserving. I have made up untruth that isn't real. I have made up all illusions. I have made up this lie, this pretense and this fiction. I can only be love light and joy.

I stop imagining my own demise. I stop imagining guilt. I stop imagining I am not love. I stop pretending to die. I suffer no more for guilt is gone. Fear is wholly undone. Sin never was at all. Separation is wholly impossible. I can only be one with God. I can only be a love that is real. I can only extend creation. I can only remain in heaven as God's child. I can only allow what is true to be. I can only let God extend love. I can only produce inner peace, inner joy. I can only extend what God has created. I can only be God's Son.

I am not guilty! I am holy and innocent. I am not guilty! I live in peace. I am not guilty! I am not condemned. I am not guilty! Sin never was. I am not guilty! Love is real. I am not guilty! My Father loves me. I am not guilty! I made this all up. I am not guilty! I am free and forgiven.

I need not imagine I made something up which really has happened and can't change. I need not imagine that some other self has decided that I am unholy. I need not imagine that guilt is real or that fear is justified at all. I need not allow the ego mind to destroy what cannot be destroyed. God's love for me is permanently real. God's love lasts forever. My oneness with God is permanently real. My oneness with God ends never. I haven't accomplished separation from God. I haven't separated at all. I must still be as God created me. I must still be in God's love.

Father, thank you for not changing your mind. Thank you for being consistent. Thank you for creating me like yourself. Thank you for eternal love. Thank you for peace. Thank you for truth. Thank you for perfect togetherness. I am your Son. We are as one. I am here with you where I belong.

Chapter 29

I am happy

Peace surrounds me, love fills me, and I am happy. I am restored to who I've always been. There is nothing but happiness and celebration at the rediscovery of what is here. No longer am I alone, no longer am I in pain. Everything has been washed clean and free from illusion. There is nothing left but to be.

I am happy because there is no reason not to be. There is no sadness because peace is restored. I am joyful to be with my Father again. I am happy to be home with love. Light is everywhere and illuminates everything. Happiness shines gloriously into eternity. A very big smile wells within me. I knew it, I never left home!

I apparently went off on a journey into some strange dream I made. I seemed to wander into unusual places with weird twisted landscapes and shadows. I appeared to encounter bodies and objects and things happening and then not happening. What was that strange dream? It never was. I am fully and completely in the light of God and dreams are gone forever.

I thought I might've tiptoed away from home to find something else entirely. But I didn't get very far at all. I just entertained the idea of what it might be like, but remained where I am all along. In my mind I imagined worlds and cities, wondering about such places existing. But I never went anywhere other than here. I never went elsewhere at all.

Somehow it seemed there were tales of horror and terror and treachery and death. Peculiar death is, never ending for real. Images of things coming and going but never really being there at all. Unexplainable illusions of importance and meaning and value and purpose, all without reason or really here. My bizarre fantasy was a mistaken thought that I took seriously. How silly it was. I'm so glad it never came about. I'm so glad it never really happened.

My friend Holy Spirit, always in my mind. It's funny I've been with you all along. We've been watching this fantasy all this time and laughing at its ridiculousness. I am obviously with you and we've always been together. We sit together and laugh. You remind me I'm home, happy and in love. Let's laugh together and be.

There is nothing else other than the presence of happiness. There is nowhere else to go. We sit on the sidelines and watch from afar. Nothing is really changing. Winds of imagery sweep past without moving us. Noises are silent and still. We sit and we laugh at how impossible are illusions. Why take them seriously at all?

I don't need to become something, I am already complete. I don't need to fix something, nothing is wrong. I don't need to find something, love is the answer. I don't need to fear because love hasn't gone. I can be happy that I need nothing else. I can be happy as I am created. I can be happy that dreams are just dreams and not real. I can be happy and joyful with love.

I am naturally joyful, I don't need to build it. I am naturally playful, I don't need to practice. I am naturally love-filled, I don't need increase it. I am naturally safe, I don't need protection. I am naturally happy, I don't need to strive. I am naturally present, I don't need to focus. I am naturally here, I don't need pretend. I am naturally as God created me.

Dreams are ridiculous. Dreams are undone. Dreams are not real. Dreams are made up. Dreams are forgiven. Dreams are bizarre. Dreams make no sense. Dreams are no more. I am filled with lightness and I carry no weight. I am filled with light and have reason to smile. I am filled with light and enjoy being love. I am filled with light, one with God.

Everything is solved. Everything is corrected. Everything is perfect. Everything is in place. I see with the vision of Holy Spirit. I see dreams in their proper light. They're obviously impossible. They're obviously fake. They have no meaning at all. They're obviously an illusion. They obviously aren't happening. They're obviously just made up pretense.

I've run out of problems. I've run out of fears. I've run out of reasons for unhappiness. I've run out of hate. I've run out of death. I've run out of reasons to be guilty. I've run out of lies. I've run out of hurt. I've run out of distortions of ego. I've run out of lack. I've run out of danger. I've run out of worry and demise. All I can be is the love God created. All I can be is True Self. All I can be is peace, light and happiness. All I can be is love.

I am already the love that God created. I am already created with light. I am already free from illusions. I am already one with God. I am already at peace and at home. I am already very happy. I am already playing with God. I am already knowing love. I am already completely satisfied. I am already fulfilled. I am already restored to sanity. I am already still.

All is forgiven, nothing has happened. All is forgiven in love. All is released, nothing has happened. All is forgiven in love.
All is joy, nothing has happened. All is forgiven in love. All is beautiful, nothing has happened. All is forgiven in love. There is nothing wrong with me. I am not at fault. I am not faulty at all. I am not defective. I am not broken. I have no reason to fall.

I am joined with you Father, I am joined in your love, I am joined - I already am. I am here with you Father, I am here in your love, I am here - I already am. I am happy with you Father, I am happy with your love, I am happy - I already am. I am at peace in you Father, I am peaceful in love, I am peaceful - I already am.

I am happy because God is very happy. I am happy because love is happiness. I am happy because my Father loves me. I am happy because I extend love and happiness. I am happy because there is only reason to laugh. I am happy because joy is my nature. I am happy to be just as God created. In happiness we are all as one.

Chapter 30

I am love

Love is. Love is all there is. Love is true. Love is life. Love is here. Love is now. Love is heaven. Love is forever. Love is endless. Love is within me. Love is around me. Love is my being. Love is who I am.

So many roads led me from love. So many paths to choose from. None of the choices gave me myself. None of them replaced who I am. Some of the paths, forgiveness and light, showed me the way back to love. But none of the paths made me the love that I am. I already am love and light.

Love is all there is. Love is what God is made of. Love extends from God forever. I am the extension of love. Love is in me. Love is through me. Love is my union with my Father. Love begins me. Love restores me. Love is my whole reality. Love flows me. Love knows me. Love shows me love. Love is here. Love is dear. Love is all there is.

Love is my completion. Love is my home. Love is the location of my Self. Love is the sanity I know. Love is my truth. Love is my life. Love is true to me. Love is here for me. Love lifts me high beyond hatred. Love joins me with love. Love welcomes me to love. Love allows me to be love.

Beautiful beloved Holy Spirit, radiant extender of love. You are love in my mind, my heart and my soul. You've always been here to love me. You know me as love. You see me with love. You restore me to love completely. You've guided me with love. You've shown me I am love. You represent love completely. Extend God's love through me to others. Help me be an example of love. Love is all I am and need to be. I share our Father's love freely.

Love is all I am meant to be. Love is all I must do. Love is my function to be only love. Love is my total companion. Love is my identity. Love is my home. Love is my family and friend. Love is my being. Love is my life. I am filled only with love. Love directs me. Love protects me. Love shows me only love. Love reminds me there is only love. Love brings me holy contentment.

I am love itself. I am created from love. I am totally love forever. Love is my savior. Love is my peace.

Love is secure and strong. Love holds me. Love heals me. Love lifts me into the heavens. Love reveals I am surrounded with love. Love shows me only what's real. Calls for love require only love. Love answers yearning for love. Absence of love is filled wholly with love. Love is the answer I need.

I am a reflection of God's love. I am God's loving Son! I extend God's love to radiate more love. God's love is where I belong. I further the presence of love from my Father. I further the presence of hope. I further the truth that love is the answer. I express only love now I am love. The love in me is the presence of my Creator. The love in me is strong. The love in me is powerful and safe love. This love can do no wrong.

Father of love, shine your love. Reveal your truth to me. Creator of love, be your love. Help me with love to see. Extender of love, flow your love. Flow your love through me. Sacred love, permanent love. Your love is all I can be.

All is restored to permanent love. All is restored to peace. All is restored to absolute heaven. All is complete, all is free. All is rejoicing and happy in love. All are blessed with love's ease. All is together and equally loved. All that is love can be.

I am this love. I am God's love. I am the love I see. I am free to love. I am free to be. I am free to be free with glee. There is nothing else. There is nowhere else. There is nothing else to be. I am only love. I am only free. I am only as God created me.

God is here. God is present. God is here with me now. God is in me. God is loving me. I allow God to love me now. I am loved by God. I am understood. I am accepted and loved and complete. I do have meaning in the eyes of Love. I am beyond any doubt that God sees me. God is here. God is loving me. God is the glow of happiness. God is beautiful. God gives me life. God knows I am love and God loves me.

I really am love. I really am alive. I really am happy and at peace. I really can be as Holiness creates me. I really am innocent and free. I really am forgiven. I really am loved. I really am one and happy. I really am the love that Love has shared. I really am love. I am free.

Thank you Holy Spirit.

Made in the USA
Las Vegas, NV
15 August 2021